I0605767

ANIMAL ENCYCLOPEDIAS

THE ASIAN ANIMAL ENCYCLOPEDIA

BY RITTA M. BASU

Encyclopedias

An Imprint of Abdo Reference

abdobooks.com

TABLE OF CONTENTS

WELCOME TO ASIA

Asia is the world's biggest continent. It covers one-third of Earth's surface, or 17.2 million square miles (44.5 million sq km). Six in ten of all humans live in Asia. India is the most populated country in the world, with 1.4 billion people. The world's most populated urban area, Tokyo, Japan, is also in Asia. It has 37 million residents.

Siberian ibex

Snow leopards

Asia has four major landforms: mountains, plains, steppes, and plateaus. Freshwater rivers, such as the Yangtze and Ganges, flow through the land, which is surrounded by the Arctic, Pacific, and Indian Oceans. Asia is home to Earth's highest mountain range, the Himalayas. In northern Asia, the Siberian plains cover the land. The Gobi Desert sprawls across the east. The Pacific Ring of Fire, known for its earthquakes and volcanoes, lines Southeast Asia.

Asia has an array of natural habitats, which include the snowy peaks of the Himalayas and the lush rainforests of Southeast Asia. A wide variety of plants and animals, such as tigers, pandas, monkeys, and elephants, live in the rainforests. The Gobi Desert is home to creatures such as the Bactrian camel, and the Siberian tundra supports species such as the Siberian musk deer. The rivers sustain unique aquatic life.

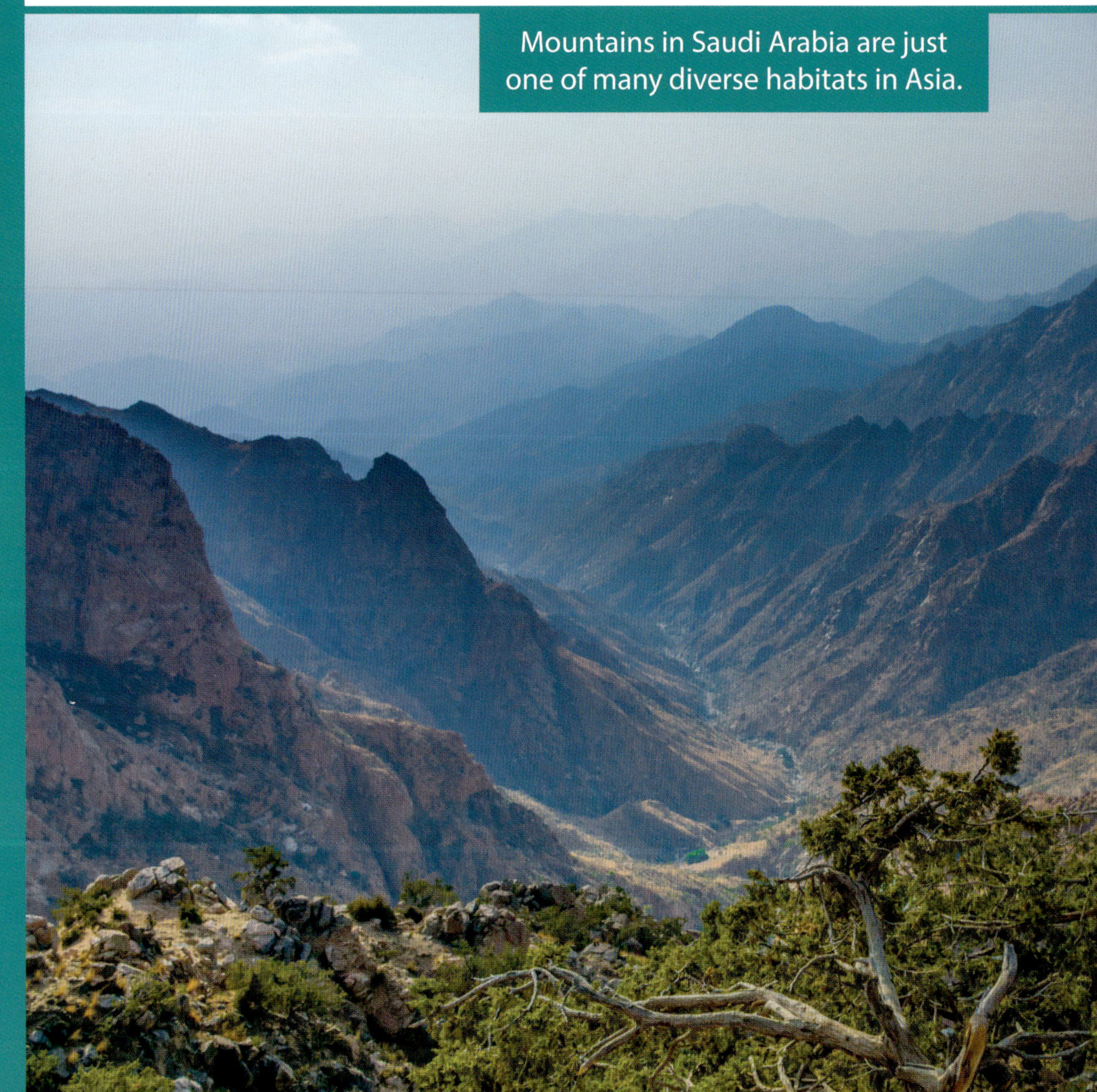

Mountains in Saudi Arabia are just one of many diverse habitats in Asia.

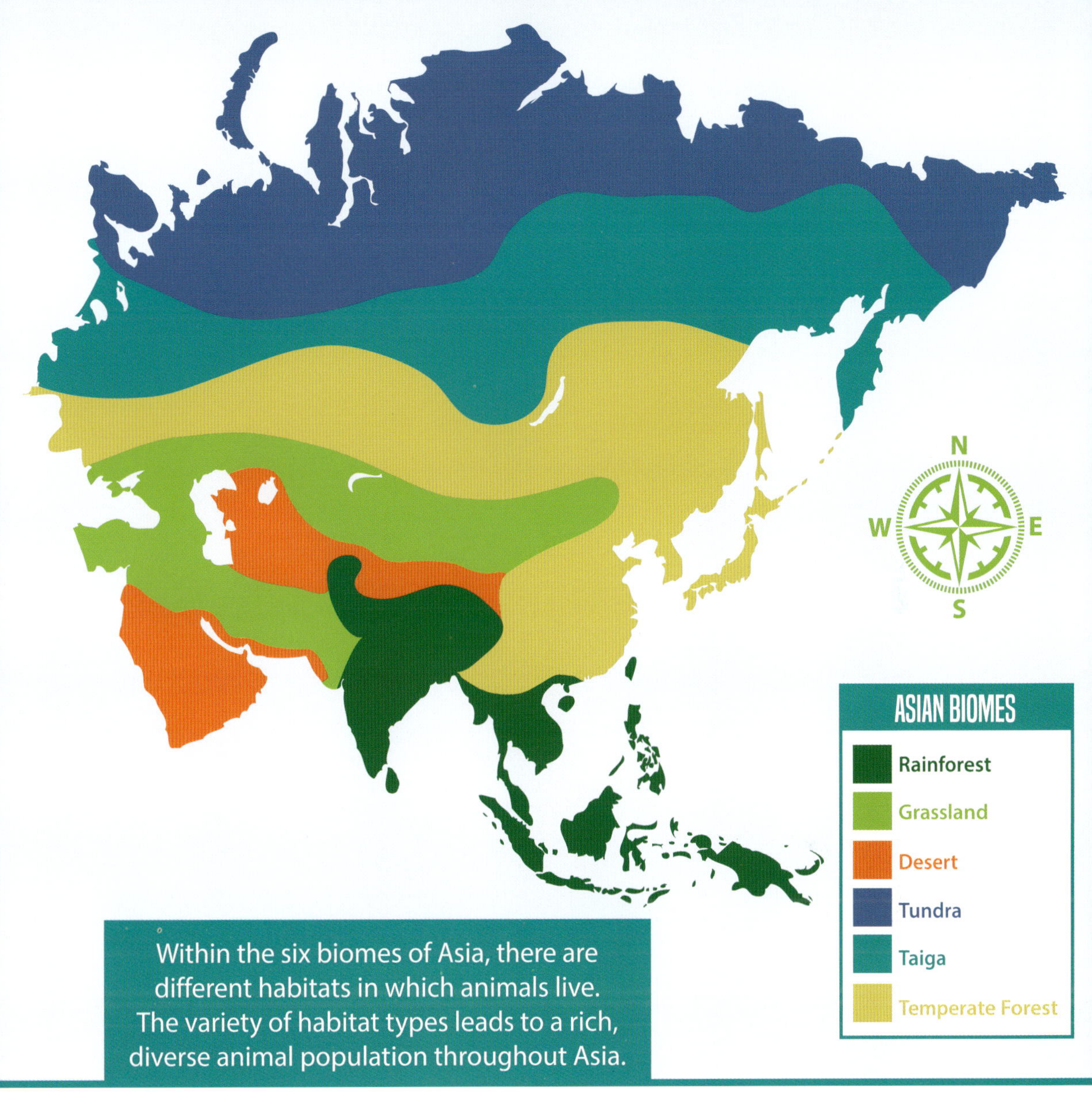

Within the six biomes of Asia, there are different habitats in which animals live. The variety of habitat types leads to a rich, diverse animal population throughout Asia.

Much like its landforms and habitats, Asia boasts a wide range of climatic conditions from cold and snow in the mountains to monsoons, typhoons, and cyclones in the tropical regions. Most of Asia's rain falls in the warm summer months, which can be hot and humid. In the coldest regions, only a limited number of species can survive.

MAMMALS

Sloth bears suck up termites and other insects easily because they have a long snout and no upper front teeth.

Asia is home to a variety of mammals, such as leopards, bears, and rhinos. Many of the continent's mammals are endemic. They are found only in Asia. These include pandas, orangutans, and tigers.

Mammals are unique in the animal kingdom. All mammals have hair or fur, even though some only have a scarce amount.

For many mammals, hair or fur helps provide warmth. Mammals are warm-blooded. Their body temperature stays the same and does not vary with the temperature of the environment. Mammals are vertebrates, meaning they have a backbone. They also have lungs to breathe air.

Most mammals give birth to live babies instead of laying eggs. Mothers feed their babies with milk produced by mammary glands.

Siberian musk deer males grow long teeth for display instead of antlers.

ASIAN SMALL-CLAWED OTTER

ALL ABOUT

The Asian small-clawed otter is the smallest otter. It uses its webbed feet and small claws to find food beneath rocks and sand in the water. Its ears and nose close when swimming.

- **Length:** 2 feet (0.6 m)
- **Weight:** up to 10 pounds (4.5 kg)
- **Lifespan:** 12 years (under human care)
- **Conservation Status:** Vulnerable

HABITAT & DIET

The small-clawed otter eats hard-shell sea creatures, such as shrimp and shellfish. They live near water, including marshes, lakes, rivers, streams, and mangrove forests in areas of southern Asia.

FAMILY & SOCIAL LIFE

These otters live in groups of 15 to 20 animals. They are vocal and communicate through sound, movement, or scent.

DID YOU KNOW?

Asian small-clawed otters dig burrows called holts into the mud, where they give birth and raise pups.

BAIKAL SEAL

ALL ABOUT

One of the smallest seals, Baikal seals have a gray coat and large eyes. These seals can hold their breath for up to 43 minutes while diving underwater.

- **Length:** 3.7 to 4.7 feet (1.1 to 1.4 m)
- **Weight:** 139 to 154 pounds (63 to 69.9 kg)
- **Lifespan:** 52 to 56 years
- **Conservation Status:** Least Concern

HABITAT & DIET

Baikal seals live in Russia's Lake Baikal, which is located in Siberia. Their main food source is the golomyanka fish.

FUN FACT

The Baikal seal is the only seal that lives completely in fresh water.

FAMILY & SOCIAL LIFE

Pups are born with a white coat and are fed by their mother. They spend a few months living in lairs that have been hollowed out on the ice. Adult seals live alone but will gather around breathing holes.

CHINESE RIVER DOLPHIN

ALL ABOUT

The Chinese river dolphin, sometimes called the Yangtze River dolphin or baiji, is thought to be extinct. None have been seen in more than 20 years.

- **Length:** 7.6 to 8.4 feet (2.3 to 2.6 m)
- **Weight:** up to 370 pounds (167.8 kg)
- **Lifespan:** 24 years
- **Conservation Status:** Extinct

DID YOU KNOW?

Chinese river dolphins had a distinct long and narrow rostrum (snout).

HABITAT & DIET

Commercial fishing, overpopulation, and noise pollution around the Yangtze River made it difficult for these dolphins to find enough freshwater fish to eat.

FAMILY & SOCIAL LIFE

While living, the river dolphins traveled together in pairs or groups.

GANGES RIVER DOLPHIN

ALL ABOUT

Ganges River dolphins have long bodies and rostrums.

- **Length:** 7.5 to 8.5 feet (2.3 to 2.6 m)
- **Weight:** 200 pounds (90.7 kg)
- **Lifespan:** 26 years
- **Conservation Status:** Endangered

HABITAT & DIET

This dolphin lives in rivers around India. It eats medium-sized fish and crustaceans from the deepest part of rivers.

FAMILY & SOCIAL LIFE

These dolphins generally travel the rivers alone, though they sometimes gather in groups.

ASIAN ELEPHANTS

ALL ABOUT

The Asian elephant is the largest land mammal on the Asian continent. They are known to be intelligent and gentle creatures. Asian elephants have rounded ears that are smaller than the ears of African elephants. There are four subspecies of Asian elephants: Indian, Bornean, Sri Lankan, and Sumatran.

FUN FACT

Most female elephants and some males develop small tusks, called tushes.

- **Height:** 6 to 10 feet (1.8 to 3 m)
- **Weight:** 5,500 to 13,200 pounds (2,494.8 to 5,987.4 kg)
- **Lifespan:** 50 years
- **Conservation Status:** Endangered

Indian elephant

HABITAT & DIET

Asian elephants live in forests, grasslands, and swamps in parts of South and Southeast Asia. As herbivores, their diet consists mostly of grasses and sometimes fruit and vegetables. Asian elephants eat up to 330 pounds (149.7 kg) of food and drink 50 gallons (189.3 L) of water daily.

FAMILY & SOCIAL LIFE

Asian elephants live in herds of six to seven adult females along with their offspring. Adult males are mostly solitary.

Elephants are social animals. They use sound, body language, and touch to communicate. Elephants can hear certain low-pitched sounds from 2 miles (3.2 km) away.

Bornean elephant

Sri Lankan elephant

DID YOU KNOW?

Sumatran elephants use tools like sticks to scratch themselves or to reach food high in trees.

ASIAN BLACK BEAR

ALL ABOUT

Asian black bears have shaggy dark fur with a white patch on their chest. They are known for their tree-climbing abilities.

- **Length:** 47.2 to 70.9 inches (119.9 to 180.1 cm)
- **Weight:** 143.2 to 330.4 pounds (65 to 149.9 kg)
- **Lifespan:** 25 years
- **Conservation Status:** Vulnerable

HABITAT & DIET

Asian black bears live in mountains and forests in many countries of Asia. They are mostly nocturnal feeders and will sleep in caves or hollow trees during the day. Their omnivorous diet includes insects, fruit, nuts, small animals, and birds.

FAMILY & SOCIAL LIFE

Cubs stay with their mother for up to three years. Otherwise, these bears are mostly solitary.

FUN FACT

Asian black bears like to sit in a nest of broken twigs and branches while they eat.

EURASIAN BROWN BEAR

ALL ABOUT

Eurasian brown bears are known for their thick coat and their ability to run and swim well.

- **Length:** 6 to 8 feet (1.8 to 2.4 m)
- **Weight:** 300 to 800 pounds (136 to 362.9 kg)
- **Lifespan:** 20 to 30 years
- **Conservation Status:** Least Concern

HABITAT & DIET

These bears adapt well and live in deserts, mountains, and icy plains of central Asia and Siberia. They live on a diet of fruit, nuts, and small mammals.

FAMILY & SOCIAL LIFE

Cubs are born during the winter hibernation period. They stay with their mother for two to four years.

DID YOU KNOW?

Eurasian brown bears used to eat mostly meat. However, due to lack of food, their diet has changed to being more plant-based.

GIANT PANDA

ALL ABOUT

The giant panda is known for its black-and-white coloration. They have no natural predators. Rather, habitat loss is the greatest threat to the survival of this species.

- **Length:** 4 to 6 feet (1.2 to 1.8 m)
- **Weight:** up to 250 pounds (113.4 kg)
- **Lifespan:** 15 to 20 years
- **Conservation Status:** Vulnerable

HABITAT & DIET

Giant pandas live in the mountainous bamboo forests of southwest China. The bears spend up to 16 hours a day eating bamboo, their primary source of food. Because bamboo is low in nutrients, giant pandas consume up to 100 pounds (45.4 kg) of it daily.

FAMILY & SOCIAL LIFE

Giant pandas have limited social interactions. They use scent marks and calls to communicate. To avoid confrontation, pandas mark their territory by rubbing their rumps on trees and the ground.

Giant pandas have a slow reproduction rate. Over her lifetime, a female may only successfully raise five to eight cubs. Newborns only weigh 3 to 5 ounces (85 to 141.7 g) and are born blind and hairless.

FUN FACT

China is the only country where pandas live in the wild.

DID YOU KNOW?

The giant panda's large wristbone acts like a thumb, helping the bear grasp and break bamboo stems.

SLOTH BEAR

ALL ABOUT

Sloth bears are not related to sloths, nor are they slow moving. These bears can run fast and climb trees. They have dark fur and often have a white patch on their chest. Sloth bears can stand on two legs to defend themselves against predators.

- **Length:** 5 to 6 feet (1.5 to 1.8 m)
- **Weight:** 200 to 300 pounds (90.7 to 136 kg)
- **Lifespan:** 16 years
- **Conservation Status:** Vulnerable

HABITAT & DIET

Sloth bears live in the grasslands and forests of southern Asia and India. They eat termites and other bugs as well as fruit.

FUN FACT

Sloth bears often carry their babies on their back.

FAMILY & SOCIAL LIFE

Sloth bears tend to be solitary but can sometimes be seen in small groups. Unlike other bears, sloth bears do not hibernate.

SUN BEAR

ALL ABOUT

Named for the golden patch of fur on its chest, the sun bear is the world's smallest bear.

- **Length:** 3.5 to 4.5 feet (1.1 to 1.4 m)
- **Weight:** 60 to 150 pounds (27.2 to 68 kg)
- **Lifespan:** 30 years (under human care)
- **Conservation Status:** Vulnerable

DID YOU KNOW?

Sun bears build nests on tree branches for resting.

HABITAT & DIET

Sun bears live in dense forests of Southeast Asia, spending much of their time in the trees. Also known as the honey bear, the sun bear uses its long tongue to get honey from beehives. It also eats insects and fruit.

FAMILY & SOCIAL LIFE

Sun bears are born without a sense of smell. As adults, they use scent and some sounds to communicate with other bears.

CORSAC FOX

ALL ABOUT

The corsac fox climbs fast but runs slowly. It relies heavily on its senses and pale-colored fur to survive in its habitat.

- **Length:** 19.7 to 23.6 inches (50 to 59.9 cm)
- **Weight:** 6.6 to 8.8 pounds (3 to 4 kg)
- **Lifespan:** 9 to 13 years
- **Conservation Status:** Least Concern

HABITAT & DIET

The corsac fox lives in grasslands and deserts of central and northeastern Asia. It eats small mammals, insects, and vegetation. The foxes make shallow holes where they sleep during the day. In the winter, they live in nests built by other animals.

FAMILY & SOCIAL LIFE

The foxes mate for life and share parenting responsibilities. Sometimes they join packs to hunt and find shelter. Mother foxes share the birthing den with other mothers.

DID YOU KNOW?

In winter, corsac foxes follow antelope who make a clear path by packing down the snow.

DHOLE

ALL ABOUT

Dholes are reddish-brown dogs that live in tight-knit packs, known for their exceptional teamwork during hunts.

- **Length:** 3 feet (0.9 m)
- **Weight:** 22 to 44 pounds (10 to 20 kg)
- **Lifespan:** 10 years
- **Conservation Status:** Endangered

HABITAT & DIET

Dholes can adapt to several habitats, including forests and alpine regions, in eastern and southern Asia. They live in burrows with multiple entrances. They are carnivores that commonly eat deer, birds, and rodents.

FUN FACT

The first domestic dogs came from Asia.

FAMILY & SOCIAL LIFE

Packs of 5 to 12 dogs hunt, eat, and care for pups together. Dholes have several sounds, including whistles, to help them hunt and communicate.

GOLDEN JACKAL

ALL ABOUT

The golden jackal is recognized by its golden-colored coat and distinct calls.

- **Length:** 27.6 to 33.5 inches (70.1 to 85.1 cm)
- **Weight:** 17.6 to 22 pounds (8 to 10 kg)
- **Lifespan:** 8 to 16 years
- **Conservation Status:** Least Concern

FUN FACT

Golden jackal pairs howl in unison as a demonstration of their lifelong bond.

HABITAT & DIET

Golden jackals live in the valleys of forests and scrubland in southern Asia. They eat hooved animals such as gazelles and deer, as well as rabbits, birds, frogs, and insects.

FAMILY & SOCIAL LIFE

Golden jackals live in groups consisting of a mated pair and its young. Female jackals don't allow other females to approach their male mate. Jackal pups stay with the parents for a year or more to help raise the next litter.

GRAY WOLF

ALL ABOUT

The gray wolf is a carnivore, known for its intelligence, teamwork, and adaptability. It is the largest member of the canine species.

- **Length:** 3 to 5 feet (0.9 to 1.5 m)
- **Weight:** 60 to 145 pounds (27.2 to 65.8 kg)
- **Lifespan:** 10 to 12 years
- **Conservation Status:** Least Concern

HABITAT & DIET

Gray wolves live in forests, wetlands, pastures, and mountains throughout much of Asia. They hunt and eat hooved animals such as elk, moose, and deer. They will also eat smaller animals and plant matter.

DID YOU KNOW?

Wolves can walk as much as 124 miles (199.6 km) per day.

FAMILY & SOCIAL LIFE

Wolves live and work together in packs of 6 to 10. A pack is led by an alpha male and female, which are the only ones to breed. Wolves communicate through barks, whines, howls, and growls.

AMUR LEOPARD

ALL ABOUT

The Amur leopard is native to eastern Russia and northeastern China. Poachers have almost destroyed the population. Only a few hundred of these cats remain in the wild.

- **Length:** 42 to 54 inches (106.7 to 137.1 cm)
- **Weight:** 70 to 105 pounds (31.6 to 47.6 kg)
- **Lifespan:** 10 to 15 years
- **Conservation Status:** Critically Endangered

DID YOU KNOW?

The surface of an Amur leopard's tongue is sharp, helping it to scrape meat from bones.

HABITAT & DIET

Amur leopards live in mountain forests in cold regions, where they use strong vision and sharp hearing to stalk prey, then pounce. They kill their prey by biting it on the neck.

FAMILY & SOCIAL LIFE

These cats are mostly solitary, but mothers help their cubs until they can fend for themselves.

ASIATIC LION

ALL ABOUT

Asiatic lions are smaller than African lions and have a shorter mane. Additionally, Asiatic lions are differentiated by long folds of skin along their belly.

- **Length:** 4.9 to 6.9 feet (1.5 to 2.1 m)
- **Weight:** 242 to 418.9 pounds (109.8 to 190 kg)
- **Lifespan:** 17 to 18 years
- **Conservation Status:** Vulnerable

HABITAT & DIET

Asiatic lions used to live across Asia, but due to hunting and habitat loss, the few hundred that remain can only be found in the Gir Forest of India. They eat mostly deer, antelope, and wild boar.

FAMILY & SOCIAL LIFE

Asiatic lions live in small prides. Male Asiatic lions usually only join a pride for mating or eating a large kill. Female lions do all the hunting.

FUN FACT

Asiatic lions are only active four hours per day.

CLOUDED LEOPARD

ALL ABOUT

Clouded leopards are smaller than most big cats. Their coats are brown or gray with dark markings. They have long canine teeth and large feet that help them climb trees.

- **Length:** 23.6 to 43.3 inches (59.9 to 110 cm)
- **Weight:** 24 to 50 pounds (10.9 to 22.7 kg)
- **Lifespan:** 12 to 15 years
- **Conservation status:** Vulnerable

HABITAT & DIET

This stealthy cat hunts in the tropical forests of India and China. During the day, clouded leopards mostly rest in trees. They hunt deer, squirrels, and birds at night.

DID YOU KNOW?

Clouded leopards can rotate their hind feet, which helps them to go down trees headfirst.

FAMILY & SOCIAL LIFE

A clouded leopard remains alone, except when mating or raising cubs.

EURASIAN LYNX

ALL ABOUT

The largest of all lynxes, the Eurasian lynx has a thick coat that is gray, reddish, or yellow with dark stripes and spots. But its tufted ears may be this feline's most distinctive feature.

- **Length:** 31 to 43 inches (78.7 to 109.2 cm)
- **Weight:** up to 84 pounds (38 kg)
- **Lifespan:** up to 17 years
- **Conservation Status:** Least Concern

HABITAT & DIET

The Eurasian lynx lives in the mountains and forests of central Asia and Russia. It mostly eats hooved mammals such as deer. It will also eat rabbits, birds, and rodents.

FAMILY & SOCIAL LIFE

These lynx are solitary except during breeding. They communicate by sound and scent.

FUN FACT

Large, padded feet allow the Eurasian lynx to quietly stalk its prey before attacking.

FISHING CAT

ALL ABOUT

Fishing cats have a stocky body and short legs. They have partially webbed feet and can swim long distances. Their flattened tail helps navigate through the water.

- **Length:** 34 to 45 inches (86.4 to 114.3 cm)
- **Weight:** up to 31 pounds (14.1 kg)
- **Lifespan:** 12 years
- **Conservation Status:** Vulnerable

HABITAT & DIET

Fishing cats are found primarily in wetlands in southern Asia. These cats mainly eat fish. They may also eat frogs, insects, birds, and sometimes rats or snakes.

DID YOU KNOW?

Fishing cats have been known to swim underwater to grab ducks' legs.

FAMILY & SOCIAL LIFE

One male fishing cat may breed with several females. Babies are born in the warmer months and are independent of their parents by 10 months old.

INDIAN LEOPARD

ALL ABOUT

Indian leopards are strong, solitary predators. Their spots, or rosettes, are bigger than any other leopard. They are fast climbers and strong swimmers.

- **Length:** 3.3 to 4.6 feet (1 to 1.4 m)
- **Weight:** 64 to 170 pounds (29 to 77.1 kg)
- **Lifespan:** 12 to 17 years
- **Conservation Status:** Vulnerable

FUN FACT

An Indian leopard can carry a dead animal more than twice its weight.

HABITAT & DIET

Indian leopards live in forests in India, Nepal, and Bhutan. They hunt during the day and are camouflaged in the trees at night. Indian leopards often drag their prey up a tree. This prevents other predators from stealing it.

FAMILY & SOCIAL LIFE

Indian leopards only socialize during mating and when raising cubs.

PALLAS'S CAT

ALL ABOUT

Pallas's cats look like domestic cats, but they are wild. They have a round face and thick fur, which protects them in cold temperatures. Their sharp claws help them climb and dig.

- **Length:** 20 to 26 inches (50.8 to 66 cm)
- **Weight:** 5.5 to 9.9 pounds (2.5 to 4.5 kg)
- **Lifespan:** 8 to 9 years
- **Conservation Status:** Least Concern

DID YOU KNOW?

Part of the scientific name of Pallas's cat, *Otocolobus*, means "ugly eared."

HABITAT & DIET

Pallas's cats are skilled hunters, preying on small rodents such as pika and gerbils, as well as birds and insects. They ambush their prey. They live in grasslands, deserts, and rocky areas of central Asia. They hide in caves, rock crevices, or abandoned burrows.

FAMILY & SOCIAL LIFE

Pallas's cats are solitary animals that leave their mother within a year.

SNOW LEOPARD

ALL ABOUT

Snow leopards have thick gray fur with dark rosettes, allowing them to expertly blend in with their surroundings. Their long, thick tail provides balance as well as warmth while sleeping.

- **Length:** 39 to 51 inches (99.1 to 129.5 cm)
- **Weight:** 77 to 121 pounds (34.9 to 54.9 kg)
- **Lifespan:** 10 to 13 years
- **Conservation Status:** Vulnerable

HABITAT & DIET

The snow leopard lives in the high, cold mountains of central and southern Asia. They primarily eat blue sheep and ibex. They also eat small animals such as marmots and rodents. They are known to be shy and elusive.

FUN FACT

Due to its excellent camouflage abilities, the snow leopard is often called the ghost cat of the Himalayas.

FAMILY & SOCIAL LIFE

These solitary cats mark their territory with heavy scents to avoid each other. They communicate by meowing and growling.

TIGERS

ALL ABOUT

Well-known to Asia for their distinctive stripes, tigers are fierce predators with large canines and claws that are up to 4 inches (10.2 cm) long. Tigers once roamed all of Asia. Hunting and habitat loss are the tiger's greatest threats.

- **Length:** 4.8 to 9.5 feet (1.5 to 2.9 m)
- **Weight:** 165 to 716 pounds (74.8 to 324.8 kg)
- **Lifespan:** 10 to 15 years
- **Conservation Status:** Endangered or Critically Endangered

HABITAT & DIET

There are six subspecies of tigers living in different habitats, which include forests, swamps, grasslands, and snowy regions. Tigers are found in small areas of India, Russia, South Asia, and Southeast Asia. They are stalk-and-ambush hunters. A tiger

Amur tiger

Siberian tiger

may only make a kill once per week. It eats as much as it can, covers the leftovers to hide them, and returns to the kill to continue eating. A tiger's diet mostly consists of pigs and deer. Tigers are excellent swimmers and climbers.

DID YOU KNOW?

Not all tigers are orange. They can also be black with tan stripes, white and tan, or all white.

FAMILY & SOCIAL LIFE

Adult tigers are solitary. They mark territories with their scent. During mating season, tigers rub against each other to share scents. Mothers also rub against their babies. Cubs stay with their mother for two years while they learn hunting and survival skills.

AMUR TIGER

Amur tigers, also called Siberian tigers, are the largest tigers. They live in the cold forests of eastern Russia and northeastern China. They have a layer of fat and a thick coat to keep them warm.

DID YOU KNOW?

Amur tigers are the largest big cats in the world. The second largest are male African lions.

BENGAL TIGER

Bengal tigers live in the tropical forests in India and surrounding countries. There are more Bengal tigers than any other species, but these cats remain endangered with only 2,000 to 2,500 living in the wild.

Bengal tiger

INDOCHINESE TIGER

Indochinese tigers live in the jungles of Southeast Asia. Their stripes help them camouflage in their jungle habitat.

Indochinese tiger

MALAYAN TIGER

The critically endangered Malayan tiger lives only on the Malay Peninsula. There are fewer than 200 individuals living in the wild.

SOUTH CHINA TIGER

The South China tiger may now be extinct in the wild. The only known South China tigers live under human care. Their numbers decreased severely in the 20th century due to hunting.

SUMATRAN TIGER

The Sumatran tiger is the smallest tiger. It has a dark coat, which helps it hide in the shadows. Long facial fur is thought to protect its face from jungle plants.

Malayan tiger

South China tiger

Sumatran tigers

BACTRIAN CAMEL

ALL ABOUT

Bactrian camels have two humps where they store fat. Their nostrils close to block blowing sand. Two toes on each foot help them walk through the desert. There are very few Bactrian camels in the wild due to domestication, hunting, and lack of food.

- **Length:** 10 to 12 feet (3 to 3.7 m)
- **Weight:** up to 2,200 pounds (997.9 kg)
- **Lifespan:** 50 years
- **Conservation Status:** Critically Endangered

FUN FACT

Bactrian camels are prey for only one predator, the gray wolf.

HABITAT & DIET

Bactrian camels live in central Asia's rocky deserts. They eat vegetation and can go months without water.

FAMILY & SOCIAL LIFE

These camels live in caravans of between 6 and 20 individuals, including a male leader. The camels sometimes form trains hundreds of camels long.

CHEVROTAIN

ALL ABOUT

Chevrotains, also known as mouse deer, are small deer-like animals found in Southeast Asia. Mouse deer are named for their size and mouse-shaped head.

- **Height:** 12 to 13 inches (30.5 to 33 cm)
- **Weight:** up to 18 pounds (8.2 kg)
- **Lifespan:** 8 to 13 years
- **Conservation Status:** Least Concern

DID YOU KNOW?

The lesser chevrotain freezes in place when it is scared.

HABITAT & DIET

Most chevrotains roam in the forest's undergrowth during late evening and early morning. They make tunnels for resting and feeding. They eat fallen fruit, mushrooms, and leaves.

FAMILY & SOCIAL LIFE

Chevrotains don't share territory, though they may stay in pairs. Females spend most of their lives pregnant, and babies become independent in two to three months.

EQUINES

ALL ABOUT

All equines belong to the horse family. The only true wild horses are native to Africa and Asia. All other horses and donkeys are descended from them.

- **Height:** 3.3 to 5 feet (1 to 1.5 m)
- **Weight:** 440.9 to 969.2 pounds (200 to 439.6 kg)
- **Lifespan:** up to 40 years
- **Conservation Status:** Varies by species

HABITAT & DIET

Equines mostly live in open plains and eat grasses and grains. Horses spend most of their time foraging for food.

FAMILY & SOCIAL LIFE

Equines live in herds of several females and males. Many herds have a single stallion that is dominant. Young males live together in bachelor herds.

Przewalski's horse

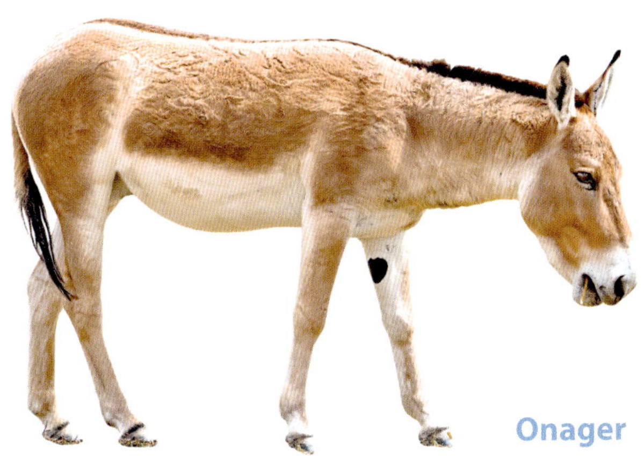

Onager

PRZEWALSKI'S HORSE

Przewalski's horses live in Mongolia, China, and Kazakhstan. They have an upright mane like a zebra's. It does not lay flat.

ONAGER

Onagers are wild donkeys that resemble horses. They are social creatures that live in small herds but sometimes gather in groups of 450 to 1,200 individuals. Onagers live in the desert plains of China and Mongolia.

KIANG

Kiang are large wild equines that live in the Tibetan Plateau. Living as family groups, they sometimes form circles with other kiang to protect themselves from wolves.

Kiang

GAUR

ALL ABOUT

Gaur, sometimes called Indian bison, are one of Asia's largest cattle species. They have large heads topped with curved horns.

- **Length:** 8.2 to 10.8 feet (2.5 to 3.3 m)
- **Weight:** 1,431.7 to 2,202.6 pounds (649.4 to 999.1 kg)
- **Lifespan:** 26 years
- **Conservation Status:** Vulnerable

FUN FACT

Gaur use loud calls to communicate.

HABITAT & DIET

Gaur are herbivores who graze mainly on grasses, trees, and bamboo in forests across Asia. They prefer to stay in the same area year-round.

FAMILY & SOCIAL LIFE

Gaur gather in herds of 8 to 11 and are active in the morning and evening. They snort and use their horns to protect themselves from predators.

MARKHOR

ALL ABOUT

The markhor is the largest species of wild goat. It is known for its large corkscrew-shaped horns.

- **Length:** 52 to 73.2 inches (132.1 to 185.9 cm)
- **Weight:** up to 242.5 pounds (110 kg)
- **Lifespan:** 11 to 13 years
- **Conservation Status:** Near Threatened

HABITAT & DIET

Markhor are native to central Asia and the Himalayas. Their strong climbing skills help them survive in their rocky, mountainous habitat. As herbivores, they eat grass, trees, and shrubs.

FAMILY & SOCIAL LIFE

Markhor live in herds of eight or nine females. Males join the herds during mating season. They use an alarm call to warn each other of predators such as snow leopards and wolves.

DID YOU KNOW?

The rings on the markhor's spiral horns tell the age of the goat.

MUSK DEER

ALL ABOUT

Deer live on every continent except Antarctica. Musk deer are small deer with grayish-brown fur. Their small size allows them to easily hide and run fast. Males have long upper teeth. These canines hang down as tusks. Musk deer do not have antlers the way most other deer species do.

- **Length:** 39.6 inches (100.6 cm)
- **Weight:** 24.3 to 39.7 pounds (11 to 18 kg)
- **Lifespan:** 12 to 20 years
- **Conservation Status:** Vulnerable or Endangered

HABITAT & DIET

As herbivores, musk deer eat vegetation such as grasses, lichens, and fruit. Musk deer live in the mountains between Siberia and the Himalayas.

FAMILY & SOCIAL LIFE

Most deer species live in herds. But some deer, such as the hog or musk deer, prefer to live alone.

REINDEER

ALL ABOUT

Reindeer can be found in the coldest parts of Asia, including northern Russia and China. They have special adaptations to help them live in the cold. Their hooves are divided into two, which helps spread their weight and allows them to stand on snow. Both male and female reindeer have antlers.

- **Height:** 28 to 53 inches (71.1 to 134.6 cm)
- **Weight:** up to 550 pounds (249.5 kg)
- **Lifespan:** 10 to 15 years
- **Conservation Status:** Vulnerable

HABITAT & DIET

Reindeer live in the Arctic tundra and in the forests of North America, Russia, and the Scandinavian countries. They eat mostly moss, herbs, grass, and the vegetation from trees.

FAMILY & SOCIAL LIFE

Reindeer live in small to large herds—up to 500,000 reindeer. They have a strong sense of smell and migrate in search of food. Their annual trek can be 3,000 miles (4,828 km) long.

RHINOCEROS

ALL ABOUT

Three different species of rhinos live in Asia: the Indian, the Sumatran, and the Javan. The Indian rhinoceros, also known as the greater one-horned rhinoceros, has the largest population of all the Asian rhinos. It is identified by a single horn, which can grow to around 10 inches (25.4 cm) long. The horn doesn't start to grow until the rhino is about six years old.

- **Length:** 10 to 13 feet (3 to 4 m)
- **Weight:** 3,968.3 to 5,511.6 pounds (1,800 to 2,500 kg)
- **Lifespan:** 40 to 50 years
- **Conservation Status:** Vulnerable

Indian rhinoceros

Sumatran rhinoceros

HABITAT & DIET

Indian rhinos live in grasslands, swamps, and forests in parts of India and Nepal. They may eat up to 19 hours and produce more than 200 pounds (90.7 kg) of dung a day. They are often found near rivers. They wallow in water and mud to cool themselves and protect their skin from insects.

FAMILY & SOCIAL LIFE

Indian rhinos usually lead solitary lives, except during mating or when females are with their calves. Calves stay with their mother until they are independent, which can be up to 10 years.

FUN FACT

Rhinoceros horns are made of keratin, the same material that is in human hair and fingernails.

DID YOU KNOW?

Indian rhinos have loose folds and lumps, called tubercles, which give their skin an armor-like appearance.

SIBERIAN IBEX

ALL ABOUT

Siberian ibex are wild goats that can be identified by their large curved horns. Their hooves have a hard outer edge surrounding a soft interior. This provides better grip, making these animals excellent climbers.

- **Length:** 4.3 to 5.6 feet (1.3 to 1.7 m)
- **Weight:** 66.1 to 220 pounds (30 to 99.8 kg)
- **Lifespan:** 17 years
- **Conservation Status:** Near Threatened

FUN FACT

The horns of the Siberian ibex can grow up to 4.9 feet (1.5 m) long.

HABITAT & DIET

These animals live in the mountains of central Asia and prefer rocky slopes and cliffs. They are herbivores, feeding on grasses, herbs, and shrubs.

FAMILY & SOCIAL LIFE

Siberian ibex usually live in small herds, with males often solitary or forming small bachelor groups outside mating season.

TAKIN

ALL ABOUT

Takins are slow moving, yet nimble mountain climbers. They are sometimes called gnu goats. A heavy coat and split hooves help them survive in the Himalayas.

- **Length:** 7.2 feet (2.2 m)
- **Weight:** up 770 pounds (349.3 kg)
- **Lifespan:** 16 to 18 years
- **Conservation Status:** Vulnerable

HABITAT & DIET

In the summer, takins live in the grass-covered mountains and migrate to the valley forests in winter. They eat a variety of vegetation. Like cows, takins ruminate their food.

DID YOU KNOW?

When a takin sleeps, it stretches out its legs and rests its head on its feet.

FAMILY & SOCIAL LIFE

Takins form herds led by a dominant male. Females give birth to only one kid each spring. Takins "cough" to signal danger then hide on the ground in bamboo thickets.

WATER BUFFALO

ALL ABOUT

The water buffalo is a large mammal, similar in appearance to an ox. It has large, curved horns and split hooves, which help it navigate wet areas without sinking.

- **Length:** 9.8 feet (3 m)
- **Weight:** 1,543.2 to 2,645.5 pounds (700 to 1,200 kg)
- **Lifespan:** up to 25 years
- **Conservation Status:** Endangered

HABITAT & DIET

Water buffalo live in swamps and forests of Southeast Asia. They graze on grasses and plants on land and in water. They communicate by making a quacking sound.

FAMILY & SOCIAL LIFE

Female buffalo stay with their mothers, whereas male buffalo leave for bachelor herds. Each mother gives birth to a single calf each year.

FUN FACT

For over 5,000 years, humans have used water buffalo for transportation and farming.

YAK

ALL ABOUT

Yaks are ox-like animals with long, shaggy hair. They are often used for work in rural areas.

- **Length:** 10 feet (3 m)
- **Weight:** 660.8 to 2,202.6 pounds (299.7 to 999.1 kg)
- **Lifespan:** up to 25 years
- **Conservation Status:** Vulnerable

HABITAT & DIET

Wild yaks live in cold, high-altitude areas or in desert steppes of the Himalayas and Tibetan Plateau. They eat grasses, leaves, moss, and other vegetation.

FAMILY & SOCIAL LIFE

Female yaks tend to live in herds and live in higher elevations to avoid predators. Males often roam alone.

GIBBON

ALL ABOUT

Gibbons are small apes with long arms and flexible wrists that allow them to swing through the trees. Gibbons walk on two legs and, like all apes, have no tail. Their coat colors range from light to dark.

Gibbons include 20 species of apes, each with its own unique characteristics. The siamang has long fingers, and hoolocks have loud vocalizations.

- **Length:** 16 to 26 inches (40.6 to 66 cm)
- **Weight:** 12 to 26 pounds (5.4 to 11.8 kg)
- **Lifespan:** 30 to 35 years
- **Conservation Status:** Endangered to Critically Endangered

Siamang

HABITAT & DIET

Gibbons live in rainforests of Southeast Asia. They primarily eat fruit, leaves, and insects.

FUN FACT

Gibbons, like other primates, groom each other as a way of bonding.

White-handed gibbon

FAMILY & SOCIAL LIFE

Gibbons are loyal to their partners and families. Each gibbon subspecies has a unique call that helps them bond and establish territories. Most gibbons are territorial and defend their home area.

DID YOU KNOW?

The siamang is the largest gibbon. The smallest is the white-handed gibbon, known for its white hands.

HAMADRYAS BABOON

ALL ABOUT

Hamadryas baboons are large-bodied monkeys. Males have silver manes and pink faces, whereas females are mostly brown.

- **Length:** 24 to 30 inches (61 to 76.2 cm)
- **Weight:** 20.3 to 47.4 pounds (9.2 to 21.5 kg)
- **Lifespan:** 37 years
- **Conservation Status:** Least Concern

HABITAT & DIET

Hamadryas baboons eat fruit, leaves, insects, and small animals. They live in the arid regions of the southern peninsula of Arabia. They are less dependent on water than other baboons.

FAMILY & SOCIAL LIFE

Groups called bands travel and eat together. Larger bands sleep and rest together. Some live in one-male units with several females.

DID YOU KNOW?

Male hamadryas baboons are twice the size of females.

LANGUR MONKEY

ALL ABOUT

Langur monkeys are a group of monkeys. Each type has a slender body, a long tail, and nimble limbs, which help it move quickly on four legs.

- **Length:** 16 to 31 inches (40.6 to 78.7 cm)
- **Weight:** 12 to 41.8 pounds (5.4 to 19 kg)
- **Lifespan:** 20 to 30 years
- **Conservation Status:** Least Concern to Critically Endangered

HABITAT & DIET

Langur monkeys live in forests and grasslands in southern Asia, India, and Southeast Asia. Some live in urban marketplaces. They eat leaves, fruit, bark, roots, and sometimes insects.

FAMILY & SOCIAL LIFE

Langurs live in troops that vary in size between 20 and 100, depending on territory and food. Females care for one another's young. Males usually leave the troop when they mature.

FUN FACT

Some langurs use their tail to communicate and signal danger.

LEAF MONKEY

ALL ABOUT

Leaf monkeys are a type of langur monkey. They have a specialized stomach for leaf digestion. Their coat helps them blend into the forests and mangrove swamp areas where they live.

- **Length:** 16 to 31 inches (40.6 to 78.7 cm)
- **Weight:** 12 to 14 pounds (5.4 to 6.4 kg)
- **Lifespan:** 20 to 30 years
- **Conservation Status:** Vulnerable

FUN FACT

Leaf monkeys have been observed playfully chasing and wrestling with each other.

HABITAT & DIET

Leaf monkeys mainly eat leaves. They also eat fruit, seeds, and blossoms. These monkeys live in Southeast Asia and spend most of their time in trees.

FAMILY & SOCIAL LIFE

One male leads a group of females and offspring. The monkeys communicate through snorts, calls, growls, and other sounds. Males protect the territories of the groups.

MACAQUE

ALL ABOUT

There are more than 20 species of macaque. They are adaptable and have larger brains than other monkeys.

- **Length:** 16 to 30 inches (40.6 to 76.2 cm)
- **Weight:** up to 39 pounds (17.7 kg)
- **Lifespan:** 20 to 30 years
- **Conservation Status:** Least Concern to Critically Endangered

HABITAT & DIET

Macaques can be found in forests, grasslands, and urban areas across Asia. Macaques eat fruit, leaves, insects, and sometimes small animals including frogs and even shrimp.

FAMILY & SOCIAL LIFE

Macaque troops can have between 4 and 100 individuals and usually include more females than males, who lead the groups. The monkeys rest and eat together and are usually social.

DID YOU KNOW?

Macaques in northern Japan often soak in natural hot springs to keep warm.

ORANGUTAN

ALL ABOUT

Orangutans are great apes with shaggy, reddish-brown fur and long arms to help them move through the trees. They are considered intelligent and have been observed using tools. Orangutans have been seen using sticks to pull insects from nests and using leaves like gloves to pick up spiky fruit.

- **Length:** 47.2 to 63 inches (119.9 to 160 cm)
- **Weight:** 66.1 to 220.5 pounds (30 to 100 kg)
- **Lifespan:** up to 58 years
- **Conservation Status:** Critically Endangered

HABITAT & DIET

Orangutans are native to rainforests of Borneo and Sumatra. However, their habitat is being lost to agricultural development, especially palm oil plantations. They mainly eat fruit but also leaves, bark, and insects. They often make a new nest each night to sleep in.

FAMILY & SOCIAL LIFE

Orangutans are mostly solitary. They communicate with long calls between each other for mating and to show dominance. Mothers only give birth once every eight to nine years. The baby stays with its mother until it is seven years old.

DID YOU KNOW?

Orangutan feet and hands look almost identical and can be used in the same ways.

PROBOSCIS MONKEY

ALL ABOUT

The proboscis monkey is named for its long nose, which is more prominent on males than females.

- **Length:** 19.7 to 27.6 inches (50 to 70.1 cm)
- **Weight:** 15 to 50 pounds (6.8 to 22.7 kg)
- **Lifespan:** 13 to 23 years
- **Conservation Status:** Endangered

HABITAT & DIET

Proboscis monkeys live in forests and swamps of Borneo. They mostly eat leaves and fruit.

FAMILY & SOCIAL LIFE

These monkeys live in small groups. A dominant male keeps away predators, while females search for food.

SNUB-NOSED MONKEY

ALL ABOUT

These monkeys have short, upturned noses and prominent cheek pouches.

- **Length:** 18 to 27 inches (45.7 to 68.6 cm)
- **Weight:** 13.2 to 33.1 pounds (6 to 15 kg)
- **Lifespan:** 20 to 30 years
- **Conservation Status:** Endangered to Critically Endangered

HABITAT & DIET

They live in mountainous forests of southern China and Southeast Asia. They eat leaves, grasses, bamboo, and fruit.

TARSIER

ALL ABOUT

Tarsiers have feet and toes meant for climbing and leaping in trees.

- **Length:** 3.5 to 7.4 inches (8.9 to 18.8 cm)
- **Weight:** 2.8 to 5.6 ounces (79.4 to 158.8 g)
- **Lifespan:** 8 to 15 years
- **Conservation Status:** Vulnerable to Endangered

HABITAT & DIET

They live in the Southeast Asian rainforests. They eat insects, snakes, and bats.

BOBAK MARMOT

ALL ABOUT

Bobak marmots have short legs and tails. Males are larger than females. These marmots hibernate half the year. When awake, they can spend up to 16 hours a day looking for food.

- **Length:** 19.3 to 22.6 inches (49 to 57.4 cm)
- **Weight:** 7.7 to 17.6 pounds (3.5 to 8 kg)
- **Lifespan:** 15 years
- **Conservation Status:** Least Concern

HABITAT & DIET

Living in underground burrows in grasslands and steppes of central Asia, this marmot eats grasses, herbs, and grains. They dig burrows to live in. These burrows create mounds on the surface of the earth.

FAMILY & SOCIAL LIFE

These marmots form colonies and eat, hibernate, and raise young together. They have a single call to signal danger to others.

DID YOU KNOW?

The bobak marmot's color changes with the seasons.

FINLAYSON'S SQUIRREL

ALL ABOUT

Finlayson's squirrels are known for their white underbelly and thick fur. They can be many different colors, including red, black, and all white. Because of this, they are also called the variable squirrel.

- **Length:** 7 to 9 inches (17.8 to 22.9 cm)
- **Weight:** 7 to 10 ounces (198.4 to 283.5 g)
- **Lifespan:** 12 years under human care
- **Conservation Status:** Least Concern

HABITAT & DIET

These squirrels live in the forests of Southeast Asia. Most of their time is spent in the trees. They eat fruit, nuts, and seeds and often store food to eat later.

FUN FACT

Finlayson's squirrels are active for more than 75 percent of their day. They spend the time hunting.

FAMILY & SOCIAL LIFE

Females give birth to one or two babies three times a year. They are raised in tree nests until maturity.

HARES

ALL ABOUT

Hares look like rabbits but are generally faster and larger. They have four toes on longer hind legs and five toes on their front feet.

- **Length:** 15 to 30 inches (38.1 to 76.2 cm)
- **Weight:** 2.2 to 8.8 pounds (1 to 4 kg)
- **Lifespan:** 6 to 9 years
- **Conservation Status:** Least Concern

Burmese hare

HABITAT & DIET

Hares are found in deserts, tundras, grasslands, and forests across Asia, feeding on grasses and plants. They tend to eat their own feces, thereby digesting their food twice. Unlike rabbits, hares do not burrow underground, instead using speed to avoid predators.

FAMILY & SOCIAL LIFE

Hares are born with fur and can see a few hours after birth. A mother spends very little time with her babies. Hares can become pregnant while they are already pregnant.

Mountain hare

BURMESE HARE

The ears on a Burmese hare can be up to 3.3 inches (8.4 cm) long.

MOUNTAIN HARE

On snowy days, mountain hares huddle together for warmth.

TAIWAN HARE

The Taiwan hare is recognized by the unique shape of its head.

Taiwan hare

JAPANESE WEASEL

ALL ABOUT

Japanese weasels are a large species of weasel. During the summer, their coats are golden, but they turn white in winter. Japanese weasels produce a strong musk to scare away threats.

- **Length:** 15.7 to 22.4 inches (39.9 to 56.9 cm)
- **Weight:** 5.3 to 15.9 ounces (150.3 to 450.8 g)
- **Lifespan:** 5 years
- **Conservation Status:** Near Threatened

HABITAT & DIET

Japanese weasels live near water in the mountains and forests of Japan. They mostly eat small mammals, birds, and insects, as well as bird eggs.

FAMILY & SOCIAL LIFE

They are solitary and defend their territory. They mark the edges of their territory using musk. Mothers raise their young in nests they build using grass and feathers.

JERBOA

ALL ABOUT

Jerboas are hopping, skipping rodents that look like tiny kangaroos. There are several species of jerboa, including the comb-toothed and long-eared jerboa.

- **Length:** 2 to 6 inches (5.1 to 15.2 cm)
- **Weight:** 1 to 2 ounces (28.3 to 56.7 g)
- **Lifespan:** 2 to 3 years
- **Conservation Status:** Least Concern

FUN FACT

Jerboas take dust baths as a way of leaving a scent.

HABITAT & DIET

They live in sandy deserts and arid regions of Asia, such as parts of Iran. They eat seeds, plants, and insects.

FAMILY & SOCIAL LIFE

Jerboas usually mate after winter hibernation and in the summer. Mothers raise two to six babies a year. They live in burrows and have excellent hearing, which helps protect them from predators.

MALAYAN PORCUPINE

ALL ABOUT

Malayan porcupines are rodents that have a coat of sharp quills to defend themselves against predators. Because of their quills, they don't have many natural predators.

- **Length:** 25 to 29 inches (63.5 to 73.4 cm)
- **Weight:** 1.5 to 5.3 pounds (0.7 to 2.4 kg)
- **Lifespan:** 27 years
- **Conservation Status:** Least Concern

HABITAT & DIET

Found in dens and burrows near rocky areas and forests in southern Asia, Malayan porcupines eat plants, roots, and fruit. They have a trail system to help them find food, including on farms.

FAMILY & SOCIAL LIFE

They generally live alone or in pairs. Usually, the female will give birth to one or two pups at a time.

FUN FACT

A baby porcupine's quills are soft. They harden as the porcupine grows.

MONGOOSE

ALL ABOUT

There are many species of mongoose. Each has a slender body, short legs, and a long tail. They are immune to snake venom and are known to kill venomous snakes.

- **Length:** 17 to 28 inches (43.2 to 71.1 cm)
- **Weight:** 0.9 to 9 pounds (0.4 to 4.1 kg)
- **Lifespan:** up to 6 to 10 years in the wild
- **Conservation Status:** Least Concern

HABITAT & DIET

Mongooses live in Southeast Asia, Sumatra, and Java. They hunt during the day. These animals eat insects, small mammals, reptiles, and sometimes eggs.

FAMILY & SOCIAL LIFE

Except when mating, most mongooses are solitary. They normally have two babies but can give birth to up to five. Some species can give birth up to three times a year.

SIBERIAN LEMMING

ALL ABOUT

Siberian lemmings have brown fur, a short tail, and small ears.

- **Length:** 3.9 to 6.3 inches (9.9 to 16 cm)
- **Weight:** 1.7 to 4.2 ounces (48.2 to 119.1 g)
- **Lifespan:** 1 to 3 years
- **Conservation Status:** Least Concern

HABITAT & DIET

In winter, the Siberian lemming lives in the Arctic tundra. In the summer, it burrows near lakes and rivers, feeding on grasses and moss. It spends most of its life under the snow.

FAMILY & SOCIAL LIFE

Siberian lemmings rarely move far from their homes. Females have two to four litters of babies each year. Some litters can include as many as 13 offspring, though the number can vary.

ZOKOR

ALL ABOUT

The zokor is a small mole-like rodent with powerful claws. It is gray to brown and has whiskers on its head. Its hearing and sense of smell are sharp.

- **Length:** 6 to 10 inches (15.2 to 25.4 cm)
- **Weight:** 6 to 12 ounces (170.1 to 340.2 g)
- **Lifespan:** 3 to 4 years
- **Conservation Status:** Least Concern

HABITAT & DIET

Zokors live in complex burrows they dig in the grasslands, meadows, and farm fields of northern China and Siberia. They mostly eat plant roots but have been known to eat insects. They store extra food underground.

DID YOU KNOW?

Zokor burrows are about 6.6 feet (2 m) underground.

FAMILY & SOCIAL LIFE

Zokors are territorial and only interact for mating. They have four or five babies in the spring that stay with their mother until autumn.

FLYING FOX

ALL ABOUT

Flying foxes are a family of bat species. They have a large wingspan of up to 5 feet (1.5 m). They do not echolocate and instead use vision to navigate.

- **Length:** 9 to 16 inches (22.9 to 40.6 cm)
- **Weight:** 1 to 2 pounds (0.5 to 0.9 kg)
- **Lifespan:** 15 to 30 years
- **Conservation Status:** Varies by species

FUN FACT

The male flying fox bites the female's neck during mating.

HABITAT & DIET

Found in tropical regions of southern Asia, the flying fox eats the fruit, nectar, and blossoms produced by trees. Some species also eat insects.

FAMILY & SOCIAL LIFE

Several hundred bats may roost in a single tree. They do not form pairs. They squawk to signal danger. Mothers often communicate with babies through touch.

KITTI'S HOG-NOSED BAT

ALL ABOUT

The world's smallest mammal, the Kitti's hog-nosed bat has a wingspan of 6 inches (15.2 cm). It is named for its pig-like snout.

- **Length:** 1.3 inches (3.3 cm)
- **Weight:** 0.07 to 0.14 ounces (2 to 4 g)
- **Lifespan:** 5 to 10 years
- **Conservation Status:** Near Threatened

HABITAT & DIET

This tiny bat roosts high in limestone caves in Thailand and Myanmar. It eats mostly insects and some spiders. They catch and eat their prey while flying.

FAMILY & SOCIAL LIFE

Bats live in colonies of up to 100 bats. Females give birth to one offspring a year. Babies are left in the cave while mothers forage for food.

DID YOU KNOW?

Kitti's hog-nosed bats are often called bumblebee bats.

MALAYAN TAPIR

ALL ABOUT

The Malayan tapir has a rounded body and an extended nose that looks like a short elephant's trunk.

- **Length:** 6 to 8 feet (1.8 to 2.4 m)
- **Weight:** 550 to 1,200 pounds (249.5 to 544.3 kg)
- **Lifespan:** 30 to 36 years
- **Conservation Status:** Endangered

HABITAT & DIET

Malayan tapirs are found in rainforests of Southeast Asia. They eat leaves, fruit, and aquatic plants and prefer to live near water. On hot days, they wallow in mud to cool down and deter biting insects.

FAMILY & SOCIAL LIFE

They live alone or in small groups, except for mating and raising young. When baby tapirs are born, their coat has stripes and spots that disappear after about six months.

FUN FACT

Tapirs cannot see well, but their hearing and sense of smell help keep them safe.

PANGOLIN

ALL ABOUT

The pangolin is the only mammal that is covered in scales. It is one of the most trafficked animals in the world. Its scales, made of keratin, are mistakenly thought to have medicinal properties.

- **Length:** 19.7 to 41.3 inches (50 to 104.9 cm)
- **Weight:** 3.5 to 72.8 pounds (1.6 to 33 kg)
- **Lifespan:** 10 to 20 years
- **Conservation Status:** Vulnerable to Critically Endangered

HABITAT & DIET

Found in forests and grasslands of Southeast Asia and China, pangolins use their long tongue and sharp claws for feeding on ants and termites, their main diet. Pangolins live in hollow trees or in underground burrows.

FAMILY & SOCIAL LIFE

Solitary and nocturnal, pangolins keep to themselves except for mating.

DID YOU KNOW?

Pups, usually born one at a time, ride on their mother's back and tail.

RED PANDA

ALL ABOUT

Red pandas have long bushy tails with black and tan rings. Their thick fur keeps them warm during the winter.

- **Length:** 20 to 26 inches (50.8 to 66 cm)
- **Weight:** 7 to 14 pounds (3.2 to 6.4 kg)
- **Lifespan:** 8 to 14 years
- **Conservation Status:** Endangered

HABITAT & DIET

Red pandas live in the forests of the Himalayas, spending most of their time in trees. Bamboo is 95 percent of their diet.

FAMILY & SOCIAL LIFE

Adults only come together to mate. Before giving birth, females build a nest inside a cave or log. The young stay in the nest until they are three months old.

FUN FACT

The red panda and the giant panda are not related.

SABLE

ALL ABOUT

The sable is a weasel-like mammal with thick dark fur that gets heavier and lighter colored during the winter.

- **Length:** 13 to 20 inches (33 to 50.8 cm)
- **Weight:** 2 to 4 pounds (0.9 to 1.8 kg)
- **Lifespan:** 8 years
- **Conservation Status:** Least Concern

HABITAT & DIET

Sables live in burrows in the mountainous forests of Russia. They mostly hunt and eat small animals.

FAMILY & SOCIAL LIFE

Sables are mostly solitary and fiercely protect their territories.

DID YOU KNOW?

Sables usually hunt in the morning and evening. They use sound and scent to find their prey.

ASIATIC CHEETAH

- **About:** There are fewer than 40 Asiatic cheetahs remaining in the wild.
- **Habitat:** desert
- **Conservation Status:** Critically Endangered

Asiatic cheetah

Bryde's whale

BRYDE'S WHALE

- **About:** These whales dive up to 984.3 feet (300 m) when hunting.
- **Habitat:** tropical and subtropical ocean waters
- **Conservation Status:** Least Concerned

DUGONG

- **About:** Dugongs mostly eat seagrass, though they may also eat algae if seagrass is scarce.
- **Habitat:** warm, shallow waters near coastlines
- **Conservation Status:** Vulnerable

Dugong

Ezo red fox

EZO RED FOX

- **About:** The Ezo red fox is native to Japan and is often in Japanese mythology.
- **Habitat:** grasslands, alpine, and urban areas
- **Conservation Status:** Least Concern

PHILIPPINE FLYING LEMUR

Philippine flying lemur

- **About:** Philippine flying lemurs can glide on thin membranes stretched between their limbs.
- **Habitat:** rainforests
- **Conservation Status:** Least Concern

Tibetan antelope

TIBETAN ANTELOPE

- **About:** Male Tibetan antelope have horns up to 23 inches (58.4 cm) long.
- **Habitat:** alpine steppe
- **Conservation Status:** Near Threatened

REPTILES

Tokay gecko

Reptiles are animals with unique features. All reptiles have scaly skin. Some reptiles, such as turtles, also have shells or scutes, which are bony plates. In addition, reptiles are vertebrates and cold-blooded. They rely on the environment to keep them warm.

Water monitor

Most reptiles reproduce by laying eggs, but some reptiles give birth to live young. When young are born or hatched, they look like miniature versions of adults. All reptiles breathe air and have lungs.

Reptiles vary greatly in appearance, behavior, and diet. They eat a variety of foods, such as meat or plants, depending on the species.

Reptiles can be found in all environments, except for places of extreme cold. Asia is home to many fascinating reptiles, including the Komodo dragon and the tokay gecko. Some Asian reptiles have special adaptations. Chameleons, for example, can change their skin color and pattern to regulate their body temperature and to camouflage themselves for protection.

King cobra

CHINESE ALLIGATOR

ALL ABOUT

The Chinese alligator has an upturned snout and is smaller than other alligators. It is the only alligator species that lives outside North or South America.

- **Length:** 4.6 to 7.2 feet (1.4 to 2.2 m)
- **Weight:** 55 to 85 pounds (24.9 to 38.6 kg)
- **Lifespan:** up to 50 years
- **Conservation Status:** Critically Endangered

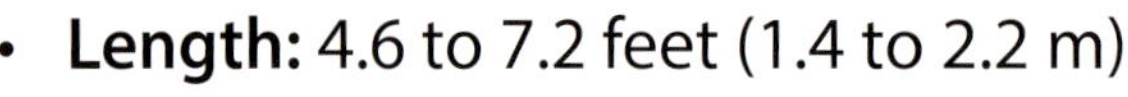

FUN FACT

Young Chinese alligators have yellow stripes on their bodies.

HABITAT & DIET

The Chinese alligator lives in the Yangtze River and other freshwater bodies in China. It eats insects, fish, crustaceans, baby waterfowl, and rodents. It digs tunnels for resting and hibernating.

FAMILY & SOCIAL LIFE

They are nocturnal animals that use sound and body movement to communicate and signal danger.

GHARIAL

ALL ABOUT

Gharials have long, narrow snouts and spend their lives in flowing rivers. Males have a round growth on the snout's end.

- **Length:** 16 to 20 feet (4.9 to 6.1 m)
- **Weight:** 350 to 550 pounds (158.8 to 249.5 kg)
- **Lifespan:** 40 to 60 years
- **Conservation Status:** Critically Endangered

HABITAT & DIET

Gharials move slowly through the deep river waters of Nepal and northern India. They hunt fish, frogs, and insects. Their vibration-sensing scales and interlocking teeth help them catch fish.

DID YOU KNOW?

Gharials have weak legs. When on shore, they slide on their belly.

FAMILY & SOCIAL LIFE

Gharials gather on riverbanks to bask in the sun for warmth. In the water, they communicate with vibrations. Mothers build nests in the sand and protect hatchlings.

MUGGER CROCODILE

ALL ABOUT

Muggers have the broadest snout of all crocodiles.

- **Length:** 7 to 16 feet (2.1 to 4.9 m)
- **Weight:** 1,541 pounds (699 kg)
- **Lifespan:** up to 28 years
- **Conservation Status:** Vulnerable

HABITAT & DIET

Mugger crocodiles live in freshwater rivers, lakes, and ponds of Southern Asia. Young muggers eat fish and crustaceans, but adults can kill large animals, including deer and tigers.

FAMILY & SOCIAL LIFE

They are solitary, territorial, and aggressive during breeding season.

DID YOU KNOW?

Muggers can chase their prey on land and in water.

SIAMESE CROCODILE

ALL ABOUT

The Siamese crocodile is almost extinct in the wild. It has olive-green scales on its sides and back and a pale stomach.

- **Length:** 6 to 10 feet (1.8 to 3 m)
- **Weight:** 110.2 to 220.5 pounds (50 to 100 kg)
- **Lifespan:** 22 years
- **Conservation Status:** Critically Endangered

FUN FACT

One Siamese crocodile can have 8,000 teeth over its lifetime, as lost teeth quickly regrow.

HABITAT & DIET

Found in fresh water across Southeast Asia, they eat fish, amphibians, and small mammals. These crocodiles wait near the water's edge to catch their prey and will occasionally eat carrion.

FAMILY & SOCIAL LIFE

These crocodiles are generally not aggressive. They communicate with loud sounds and scent.

ASIAN WATER MONITOR

ALL ABOUT

The Asian water monitor is the world's second-largest lizard. When threatened on land, it climbs trees and leaps into the water.

- **Length:** up to 9.8 feet (3 m)
- **Weight:** 43 to 110.2 pounds (19.5 to 50 kg)
- **Lifespan:** 11 years under human care
- **Conservation Status:** Least Concern

HABITAT & DIET

Asian water monitors live mainly in forests and mangrove swamps of southern Asia. They can live on land and in the water. They eat fish, birds, and small mammals.

FUN FACT

The Asian water monitor uses the fin on its tail like a paddle to steer.

FAMILY & SOCIAL LIFE

Females lay a clutch of between 10 and 40 eggs, which incubate for 6 to 7 months. The babies are fully developed when they hatch.

DRACO LIZARD

ALL ABOUT

Draco lizards are called flying dragons as they have an expanding rib cage that allows them to glide from tree to tree to find food.

- **Length:** 5 to 8 inches (12.7 to 20.3 cm)
- **Weight:** 0.2 to 0.4 ounces (5.7 to 11.3 g)
- **Lifespan:** 8 years
- **Conservation Status:** Least Concern

HABITAT & DIET

They live in the rainforests of Southeast Asia and eat only ants and termites. Their tongue flicks almost constantly as they move.

FAMILY & SOCIAL LIFE

Male lizards may claim two to three trees in the forest for themselves. Females only go to the ground to lay eggs. They guard the nest for only 24 hours after eggs are laid.

DID YOU KNOW?

Draco means "dragon" in Latin.

KOMODO DRAGON

ALL ABOUT

The Komodo dragon is the world's largest lizard. It has powerful jaws and sharp teeth, along with rugged scales that help regulate body temperature. These reptiles can take down large prey, including deer and wild boar. If prey escapes the dragon's bite, it will die from an infection caused by bacteria in the reptile's saliva.

- **Length:** 8 to 10 feet (2.4 to 3 m)
- **Weight:** up to 363.8 pounds (165 kg)
- **Lifespan:** 30 years
- **Conservation Status:** Endangered

HABITAT & DIET

Komodo dragons are native to the Indonesian islands. While hunting, dragons often lay camouflaged in bushes and grasses, waiting for prey to pass. Then the dragons pounce. In addition to large mammals, they eat smaller prey, including other reptiles and baby Komodo dragons.

FAMILY & SOCIAL LIFE

Komodo dragons are mostly solitary but often form small groups around food sources. Females lay 15 to 30 eggs, each the size of a grapefruit, and guard the nest for a short time. However, when baby dragons hatch, they are on their own.

FUN FACT

Komodo dragons eat almost all of their prey, including bones, skin, and hooves.

ORIENTAL GARDEN LIZARD

ALL ABOUT

Oriental garden lizards typically have slender, colorful bodies with long tails, which can grow up to 12 to 16 inches (30.5 to 40.6 cm). They are known for their ability to change color, which provides camouflage.

- **Length:** 15 inches (38.1 cm)
- **Weight:** 1.5 to 3 ounces (42.5 to 85 g)
- **Lifespan:** 5 years
- **Conservation Status:** Least Concern

HABITAT & DIET

Found across Asia in gardens, forests, and the undergrowth in urban areas, these lizards eat insects, small reptiles, and fruit.

FAMILY & SOCIAL LIFE

This lizard lives alone and is often hostile during mating season. A male's throat turns red during mating, and its entire head turns red after winning a battle.

DID YOU KNOW?

This animal's tail can break off if grabbed by a predator, which allows the lizard to escape while the predator is distracted by the wriggling tail. A new, but often less colorful, tail regenerates.

TOKAY GECKO

ALL ABOUT

The large tokay gecko has a robust body and sticky toe pads. Its skin is naturally gray with red spots but changes color to camouflage and avoid predators.

- **Length:** up to 16 inches (40.6 cm)
- **Weight:** up to 14 ounces (396.9 g)
- **Lifespan:** 7 to 10 years under human care
- **Conservation Status:** Least Concern

FUN FACT

It is possible to see straight through a tokay gecko's head by looking through its ears.

HABITAT & DIET

The tokay gecko is arboreal and native to the rainforests of Southeast Asia. It can also be found in human-made environments, such as homes. This gecko eats mostly insects.

FAMILY & SOCIAL LIFE

Nocturnal and solitary, the geckos may be territorial and communicate with special calls.

GOLDEN TREE SNAKE

ALL ABOUT

The golden tree snake is a rare species that can glide through the air. It kills its prey by squeezing its neck.

- **Length:** 3 to 4 feet (0.9 to 1.2 m)
- **Weight:** not enough data
- **Lifespan:** 4 to 12 years
- **Conservation Status:** Least Concern

HABITAT & DIET

Golden tree snakes are found throughout the forests of Thailand and other Asian countries. These fast-moving snakes move from tree to tree. They can also navigate rocks and other terrain. They primarily eat lizards, bats, and small mammals.

FAMILY & SOCIAL LIFE

The golden tree snake prefers solitude. Females lay clutches of 6 to 12 eggs. Babies, called snakelets, hatch in June.

INDIAN WOLF SNAKE

ALL ABOUT

The shy, alert Indian wolf snake is not venomous. It defends itself by coiling up and lashing out with its sharp fangs, which resemble those of a canine. These snakes are good climbers and swimmers.

FUN FACT

The Indian wolf snake is often mistaken for the common krait, which is highly venomous.

- **Length:** 19.7 to 27.6 inches (50 to 70.1 cm)
- **Weight:** 3.5 to 7.1 ounces (99.2 to 201.3 g)
- **Lifespan:** unknown
- **Conservation Status:** Least Concern

HABITAT & DIET

Found in forests and on farmlands in India and neighboring countries, the Indian wolf snake eats small rodents, frogs, and insects. It prefers a diet of geckos.

FAMILY & SOCIAL LIFE

This snake is nocturnal and solitary. Babies hatch from eggs and are immediately on their own.

KING COBRA

ALL ABOUT

The king cobra is the world's longest venomous snake. Its bite can kill an adult elephant.

- **Length:** 12 to 18 feet (3.7 to 5.5 m)
- **Weight:** 13 to 20 pounds (5.9 to 9.1 kg)
- **Lifespan:** 20 years
- **Conservation Status:** Vulnerable

DID YOU KNOW?

The king cobra's fangs are grooved, which allows it to deliver more venom with a single bite.

HABITAT & DIET

King cobras live in dense forests and swamps in India, China, and parts of Southeast Asia. They prefer to be near water so they can swim in search of food. They primarily eat other snakes and lizards as well as small mammals. They use their forked tongues to find food and water.

FAMILY & SOCIAL LIFE

Cobras live alone, but during mating season, males wrestle rivals for female attention.

KRAITS

ALL ABOUT

Banded krait

Kraits are venomous snakes. Their venom disables the nervous system. Kraits usually have bands of bright colors alternating with black.

- **Length:** 23.6 to 47.2 inches (59.9 to 119.9 cm)
- **Weight:** Varies by species
- **Lifespan:** up to 17 years under human care
- **Conservation Status:** Near Threatened to Vulnerable

HABITAT & DIET

They are found in woods and fields of southern Asia and Indonesia, usually near water sources. They feed on lizards, rodents, amphibians, and other snakes.

FAMILY & SOCIAL LIFE

Kraits are solitary and hunt at night. Kraits are not aggressive and usually do not attack humans unless provoked. They lay between 5 and 12 eggs on the ground. Mothers may coil themselves around the eggs to protect them.

PYTHONS

ALL ABOUT

Pythons are some of the largest snake species on Earth. Most of them have heat-sensing pits above their lips, which help them track their prey.

- **Length:** up to 30 feet (9.1 m)
- **Weight:** up to 595.2 pounds (270 kg)
- **Lifespan:** 23 to 29 years
- **Conservation Status:** Varies by species

HABITAT & DIET

Pythons live in tropical and subtropical parts of Asia. Pythons are ambush hunters and kill their prey by constricting, squeezing it to death.

FAMILY & SOCIAL LIFE

All pythons lay eggs. In most species, mothers will coil around the eggs and will shiver to produce heat. Once the eggs hatch, python babies are on their own.

Burmese python

BURMESE PYTHON

The Burmese python is one of the heaviest snakes. Baby pythons hatch by breaking the shell with their egg tooth.

INDIAN ROCK PYTHON

After eating a deer, the Indian rock python can go for months without eating.

RETICULATED PYTHON

The reticulated python is the world's longest snake and is often hunted for its skin.

Indian rock python

Reticulated python

Green pit viper

VIPERS

ALL ABOUT

All vipers are venomous snakes with long fangs. When they're not in use, these teeth fold back along the roof of their mouth. Many species of vipers have infrared sensors to sense heat.

- **Length:** 2 to 3 feet (0.6 to 0.9 m)
- **Weight:** 3.5 to 7.1 ounces (99.2 to 201.3 g)
- **Lifespan:** 10 to 15 years
- **Conservation Status:** Varies by species

HABITAT & DIET

Vipers are found all over the world. These snakes live both on the ground and in trees. They hunt by lying in wait and striking prey as it passes, disabling it with venom.

FAMILY & SOCIAL LIFE

Vipers are solitary animals and only come together to mate. Most vipers give birth to live young.

GREEN PIT VIPER

Green pit vipers live in trees but have been known to hunt on the ground at night.

INDONESIAN PIT VIPER

Indonesian pit vipers use their fangs to pull prey into their mouth.

STEJNEGER'S PIT VIPER

This viper mostly eats frogs but will also eat other animals such as mammals or birds.

FUN FACT

The venom of some vipers is used to develop new medicines.

Indonesian pit viper

ASIAN BOX TURTLE

ALL ABOUT

Asian box turtles have domed shells and three stripes that run along each side of their face. There are four subspecies, all of which are at risk.

- **Length:** 5 to 10 inches (12.7 to 25.4 cm)
- **Weight:** 1.8 pounds (0.8 kg)
- **Lifespan:** 25 to 30 years
- **Conservation Status:** Endangered

HABITAT & DIET

Found in wetlands, marshes, and rice paddies of Southeast Asia, these turtles eat plants, fruit, worms, and small invertebrates. They do not need to eat every day.

FAMILY & SOCIAL LIFE

Mothers lay two eggs three times a year. After babies hatch, they can care for themselves. Adults only socialize when they mate.

DID YOU KNOW?

Most turtles hibernate in cold weather, but because Asian box turtles live in warm climates, they are active for the entire year.

ASIAN GIANT TORTOISE

ALL ABOUT

Asian giant tortoises carry a large, heavy shell, have a long neck for reaching food, and rely on powerful legs for walking.

- **Length:** 36 to 55 inches (91.4 to 139.7 cm)
- **Weight:** 352.7 to 551.2 pounds (160 to 250 kg)
- **Lifespan:** 100 to 176 years
- **Conservation Status:** Vulnerable

HABITAT & DIET

Found in forests, swamps, and coastal areas of India, Indonesia, and Southeast Asia, they eat plants, fruit, and occasionally carrion.

DID YOU KNOW?

All giant tortoises are known to live a long life due in part to their slow metabolism.

FAMILY & SOCIAL LIFE

This giant tortoise is active in the early morning and spends the rest of the day under shade trees and burrowing in damp soil. These tortoises are usually solitary but gather in groups around food.

ASIATIC SOFTSHELL TURTLE

ALL ABOUT

Softshell turtles do not have scutes. These turtles bury themselves underwater in sand and mud to camouflage. They are strong swimmers. Asiatic softshell turtles have a snorkel-like snout used for breathing while submerged. The largest softshell turtle species in the world is the Indian softshell turtle.

- **Length:** 28 to 32 inches (71.1 to 81.3 cm)
- **Weight:** 33.1 to 66.1 pounds (15 to 30 kg)
- **Lifespan:** 20 to 30 years
- **Conservation Status:** Vulnerable

HABITAT & DIET

Softshells live in fresh water, often in rivers and streams. Some species live in brackish water near oceans. Their diet consists mostly of fish and invertebrates.

FAMILY & SOCIAL LIFE

They are mostly solitary animals and come together in the spring to mate. Some species lay only three eggs at a time, whereas others lay up to 100.

BIG-HEADED TURTLE

ALL ABOUT

The big-headed turtle has a large head relative to its body size. It is covered by a smooth, flattened shell. The shell is yellow or brown. These turtles have strong webbed claws.

- **Length:** up to 15.7 inches (39.9 cm)
- **Weight:** 0.7 to 3.3 pounds (0.3 to 1.5 kg)
- **Lifespan:** 15 to 20 years under human care
- **Conservation Status:** Critically Endangered

HABITAT & DIET

Found in fast moving fresh waters in India, Indonesia, and Southeast Asia, big-headed turtles eat aquatic plants, insects, and small fish. These turtles have strong jaws that help crush shellfish. They use their tails to navigate through the water. Their beaks and claws help them climb trees.

FAMILY & SOCIAL LIFE

Solitary and shy, this turtle has limited social interactions. Females usually lay only one or two eggs at a time.

FUN FACT

The big-headed turtle's head can't fit inside its shell, so is covered with a bony "roof" that keeps it safe.

CHINESE SOFTSHELL TURTLE

ALL ABOUT

The solitary and nocturnal Chinese softshell turtle will bury ifself in mud or sand for camouflage. They have a long snout that helps them to "snorkel" in shallow water.

- **Length:** 11 to 13 inches (27.9 to 33 cm)
- **Weight:** up to 13.2 pounds (6 kg)
- **Lifespan:** 20 to 50 years
- **Conservation Status:** Vulnerable

HABITAT & DIET

These turtles are native to China and Taiwan but can also be found throughout the world. They live mostly in fresh and inland water. They eat fish, crustaceans, insects, and some seeds.

FAMILY & SOCIAL LIFE

These turtles become mature after about five years. After mating, females can store the sperm for up to a year before laying multiple clutches of 8 to 30 eggs each year.

INDIAN STAR TORTOISE

ALL ABOUT

Named for the star-like patterns on its domed shell, the Indian star tortoise uses its strong legs for moving and digging. Females are usually larger than males.

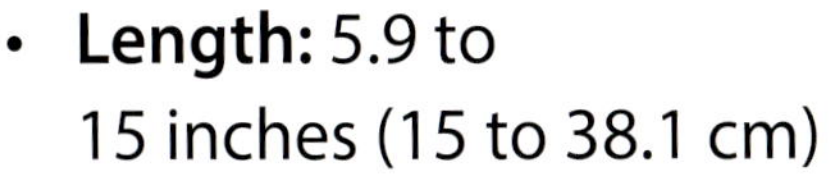

- **Length:** 5.9 to 15 inches (15 to 38.1 cm)
- **Weight:** 2 to 14 pounds (0.9 to 6.4 kg)
- **Lifespan:** 35 to 80 years
- **Conservation Status:** Vulnerable

HABITAT & DIET

Found in desert areas and scrub forests in India, the tortoise eats grasses, fruit, and flowers.

FAMILY & SOCIAL LIFE

This tortoise prefers solitude but gathers with others near food sources. They are active in the early morning and late afternoon. During the rainy season, they become more active and spend most of their time feeding.

DID YOU KNOW?

Each tortoise has its own color and arrangement of star patterns on its back.

SEA TURTLES

ALL ABOUT

Sea turtles have been around for at least 120 million years. All species have limbs that do not pull into their large, bony shells.

- **Length:** 29.5 to 84 inches (74.9 to 213.4 cm)
- **Weight:** 78.6 to 2,000 pounds (35.7 to 907.2 kg)
- **Lifespan:** 30 to 75 years
- **Conservation Status:** Varies by species

HABITAT & DIET

Sea turtles can be found in temperate ocean waters throughout the world. They come on to land to sunbathe or nest. The green turtle is the only species that eats primarily vegetation. The other sea turtle species eat vegetation as well as fish, mollusks, sponges, or jellyfish.

DID YOU KNOW?

Pollution and entrapment in fishing gear are two major threats to sea turtles' survival.

FAMILY & SOCIAL LIFE

Sea turtles migrate alone in search of food and moderate water temperature. It is believed they use magnetism to navigate. Mothers return to the beach where they were born to lay eggs.

Hawksbill sea turtle

Leatherback sea turtle

GREEN TURTLE

Green turtles are an endangered species. They are named for the color of their fat, which is green due to their diet of seagrasses and algae.

HAWKSBILL SEA TURTLE

The critically endangered hawksbill is named for its bird-like beak, which, like other sea turtles, it uses to grab and tear food.

LEATHERBACK SEA TURTLE

Leatherbacks are the largest sea turtle species. They have a soft, leathery shell.

LOGGERHEAD SEA TURTLE

Named for their large head, loggerhead turtles migrate thousands of miles annually. This species is vulnerable.

Loggerhead sea turtle

ADDITIONAL REPTILES

ASIAN SNAKE-EYED SKINK

- **About:** Snake-eyed skinks lack eyelids. Instead, their eyes are protected by scales called spectacles.
- **Habitat:** under leaf litter
- **Conservation Status:** Least Concern

Asian snake-eyed skink

Horsfield's tortoise

HORSFIELD'S TORTOISE

- **About:** Horsfield's tortoises dig burrows in the sand that can be up to 78 inches (198.1 cm) long.
- **Habitat:** dry sandy areas
- **Conservation Status:** Vulnerable

INDOCHINESE SPITTING COBRA

- **About:** These snakes have the ability to spit venom as soon as they hatch.
- **Habitat:** wide variety of habitats in Southeast Asia
- **Conservation Status:** Vulnerable

Indochinese spitting cobra

MALAYAN SNAIL-EATING TURTLE

- **About:** Female snail-eating turtles are much larger than the males.
- **Habitat:** wet lowlands
- **Conservation Status:** Least Concern

Malayan snail-eating turtle

Slug-eating snake

SLUG-EATING SNAKE

- **About:** Slug-eating snakes eat their food by sliding one side of their jaw forward at a time while holding it in place with the other.
- **Habitat:** forests
- **Conservation Status:** Least Concern

STEPPE RATSNAKE

- **About:** When threatened, steppe ratsnakes rear up and shake their tail to scare off predators.
- **Habitat:** shrubland, grasslands, and wetlands
- **Conservation Status:** Least Concern

Steppe ratsnake

BIRDS

There are more than 10,000 species of birds in the world. All birds are warm-blooded and have wings and feathers. But not all birds can fly. Some use their wings to swim or for mating displays. Birds do not have a good sense of smell, but they have strong vision and hearing and often use calls to communicate.

Steller's sea eagle

Golden pheasants

Birds lay eggs, brood the eggs, and care for their young after birth. When birds hatch, they can't see and are either featherless or have very few feathers. When baby birds start learning to fly, they are called fledglings.

Asia is home to a wide variety of birds. They live in a range of habitats, from rainforests to rivers and seashores, and in diverse climates from cold regions to dry deserts.

AMUR FALCON

ALL ABOUT

The Amur falcon is small with dark plumage, white underparts, and red legs and feet. They sometimes roost with other birds of prey.

- **Length:** 11 to 11.8 inches (27.9 to 30 cm)
- **Weight:** 3.4 to 6.6 ounces (96.4 to 187.1 g)
- **Lifespan:** 10 to 13 years
- **Conservation Status:** Least Concern

HABITAT & DIET

Every year, Amur falcons migrate in large flocks from their breeding grounds in eastern Asia to southern Africa where they spend the winter. They are found in open woodlands and grasslands, feeding on insects, small birds, and rodents.

FUN FACT

Amur falcons have one of the longest migrations of any bird, traveling more than 12,000 miles (19,312.1 km) in a year.

FAMILY & SOCIAL LIFE

Amur falcons are mostly solitary except during migration. They don't build their own nests. Instead, they use nests abandoned by other birds.

BLACK KITE

ALL ABOUT

Black kites are medium-sized raptors with finger-shaped wings and forked tails. These birds migrate to warmer climates during the winter.

- **Length:** 18 to 22 inches (45.7 to 55.9 cm)
- **Weight:** 22 to 33 ounces (623.7 to 935.5 g)
- **Lifespan:** 20 to 24 years
- **Conservation Status:** Least Concern

HABITAT & DIET

Black kites prefer areas with access to water, which is where they find their primary food of fish and insects. They are scavengers and will eat most anything, including carrion and food stolen from other birds.

FAMILY & SOCIAL LIFE

Often seen in large flocks during migration, they are solitary or in pairs during breeding.

DID YOU KNOW?

Black kites are often seen soaring over urban areas and garbage dumps in search of food.

EAGLES

ALL ABOUT

Eagles consist of more than 60 species of birds. All of them are large, powerful birds of prey. They have large beaks and feet and strong vision.

- **Length:** 26 to 41 inches (66 to 104.1 cm)
- **Weight:** 5 to 20 pounds (2.3 to 9.1 kg)
- **Lifespan:** up to 60 years
- **Conservation Status:** Varies by species

HABITAT & DIET

Eagles can be found all over the world. All eagles are carnivores and hunt for prey from the air.

FAMILY & SOCIAL LIFE

Eagles mate for life and return to the same nest each year to raise their young. It can take young eagles up to four years to reach maturity.

Japanese golden eagle

JAPANESE GOLDEN EAGLE

Japanese golden eagles can take down prey much larger than themselves, including deer and other large mammals. Their conservation status is least concern.

Philippine eagle

PHILIPPINE EAGLE

The Philippine eagle is criticially endangered. It is one of the world's heaviest eagles. Killing one of these protected birds in the Philippines could lead to a 12-year prison term.

PALLAS'S FISH EAGLE

Pallas's fish eagles are endangered. They sometimes attack other larger birds, such as ospreys and kites, and steal their food.

Pallas's fish eagle

STELLER'S SEA EAGLE

Steller's sea eagles are among the largest eagles globally, with wingspans that can reach up to 8 feet (2.4 m). The species' conservation status is vulnerable.

BARN OWL

ALL ABOUT

Barn owls have a heart-shaped face and special feathers that allow them to fly silently. Like other owls, they are nocturnal predators that capture their prey when they least expect it.

- **Length:** 12 to 16 inches (30.5 to 40.6 cm)
- **Weight:** 15.5 to 21.9 ounces (439.4 to 620.9 g)
- **Lifespan:** up to 34 years
- **Conservation Status:** Least Concern

HABITAT & DIET

Barn owls, like other owls, live on every continent except Antarctica. They eat many different prey items, including rodents, insects, reptiles, and fish.

FAMILY & SOCIAL LIFE

Most barn owls live alone or in pairs. They build nests in hollow trees or the old nests of other birds. Some owls dig burrows and raise their young on the ground instead.

SNOWY OWL

ALL ABOUT

Snowy owls have dense feathers on their legs and feet that act as insulation against freezing temperatures. Their feathers are mostly white with black dots.

- **Length:** 24.8 to 28.7 inches (63 to 72.9 cm)
- **Weight:** 3 pounds (1.4 kg)
- **Lifespan:** 10 to 28 years
- **Conservation Status:** Vulnerable

HABITAT & DIET

Snowy owls live in the polar regions of North America and the Arctic tundra. They prefer open grasslands to trees.

FAMILY & SOCIAL LIFE

Snowy owls form pairs for a breeding season. Females lay their eggs in a nest on the ground. Both males and females protect the nest from predators. They help care for the young for about four months.

BLOOD PHEASANT

ALL ABOUT

Blood pheasants get their name from the large red patch on the males' throat, chest, and forehead. These birds don't fly well but are excellent runners.

- **Length:** 15 to 22 inches (38.1 to 55.9 cm)
- **Weight:** 1 to 2 pounds (0.5 to 0.9 kg)
- **Lifespan:** 5 to 7 years
- **Conservation Status:** Least Concern

HABITAT & DIET

Found in mountainous regions of Asia, the blood pheasant prefers evergreen forests in higher elevations during the summer. In the winter, groups gather at lower elevations. They eat moss, ferns, and the needles from evergreens.

FUN FACT

The male blood pheasant's bright red plumage is used to attract females and establish dominance during mating season.

FAMILY & SOCIAL LIFE

These birds form pairs, and males defend the nest area during incubation. Both parents care for the babies.

GOLDEN PHEASANT

ALL ABOUT

Male golden pheasants have bright red, blue, and green feathers on their body. Golden head feathers spread to cover their face. Females have brown feathers.

- **Length:** 24 to 45 inches (61 to 114.3 cm)
- **Weight:** 19.4 to 24.7 ounces (550 to 700.2 g)
- **Lifespan:** 5 to 20 years
- **Conservation Status:** Least Concern

HABITAT & DIET

Found in forests and mountainous areas of China, these pheasants mostly stay on the ground but sleep in trees. They eat seeds, berries, insects, and vegetation.

FAMILY & SOCIAL LIFE

Golden pheasants mostly stay alone, except during mating. They nest on the ground. Chicks are able to feed themselves and move around after hatching.

DID YOU KNOW?

When golden pheasants get startled, they jump up quickly, sending out a warning with their wings.

HAZEL GROUSE

ALL ABOUT

The hazel grouse, sometimes called the hazel hen, has brown-and-gray feathers with flecks of white. Its coloring helps this small grouse camouflage in the forests and woodlands where it lives.

- **Length:** 11 to 13 inches (27.9 to 33 cm)
- **Weight:** 0.5 to 0.8 pounds (0.2 to 0.4 kg)
- **Lifespan:** 2 to 3 years
- **Conservation Status:** Least Concern

HABITAT & DIET

The hazel grouse is found across northern Asia and Eurasia. They eat buds, shoots, berries, and sometimes insects when breeding. They eat on the ground.

FAMILY & SOCIAL LIFE

These birds do not move much and rarely get in trees. Females nest on the ground and raise their chicks alone.

FUN FACT

The hazel grouse is known for its shy nature.

JAPANESE GROUSE

ALL ABOUT

Often called the rock ptarmigan, the Japanese grouse is referred to as "the messenger of the gods." Its feathers change with the season. This helps it stay camouflaged.

- **Length:** 14 to 18 inches (35.6 to 45.7 cm)
- **Weight:** 0.8 to 1.2 pounds (0.4 to 0.5 kg)
- **Lifespan:** 2 to 4 years
- **Conservation Status:** Least Concern

HABITAT & DIET

Found in the tundra and rocky mountain areas of Japan, these grouse eat leaves, seeds, and insects. They cannot store much fat, so they must eat frequently.

FAMILY & SOCIAL LIFE

When they are not breeding, Japanese grouse live in small flocks. They sometimes burrow in the snow to protect themselves.

DID YOU KNOW?

The Japanese grouse is commonly shown in Japanese art.

ALEXANDRINE PARAKEET

ALL ABOUT

Named after Alexander the Great, the Alexandrine parakeet has bright green feathers with patches of red on its shoulders. It is known to be an intelligent bird.

- **Length:** 22 to 25 inches (55.9 to 63.5 cm)
- **Weight:** 8.8 to 9.2 ounces (249.5 to 260.8 g)
- **Lifespan:** 25 to 30 years
- **Conservation Status:** Near Threatened

HABITAT & DIET

Found in southern Asian and Southeast Asian forests and woodlands, the Alexandrine parakeet feeds on fruit, seeds, nuts, and flowers.

FAMILY & SOCIAL LIFE

These parakeets are noisy, social birds. They live together in small flocks, which can be larger when food is abundant. Mates form close bonds with one another.

DID YOU KNOW?

Alexandrine parakeets can mimic human speech, making them popular pets.

CEYLON HANGING PARROT

ALL ABOUT

Also known as the Sri Lanka hanging parrot, the Ceylon hanging parrot is known for its green feathers, red throat patch, and acrobatic skills while hunting. It is entirely arboreal and never comes down to the ground.

- **Length:** 5.1 inches (13 cm)
- **Weight:** 1.1 ounces (31.2 g)
- **Lifespan:** 10 years
- **Conservation Status:** Least Concern

HABITAT & DIET

Found in Sri Lankan forests and plantations, the Ceylon hanging parrot feeds on fruit, flowers, and buds.

FAMILY & SOCIAL LIFE

Typically seen in pairs or small groups, these parrots nest in tree cavities. Chicks leave the nest after a month.

FUN FACT

Ceylon hanging parrots can hang upside down while eating.

INDIAN RING-NECKED PARAKEET

ALL ABOUT

The Indian ring-necked parakeet can be recognized by the thin ring around the neck in males. Sometimes called the rose-ringed parakeet, it is known for its intelligence and its ability to mimic human speech.

- **Length:** 15 to 16.5 inches (38.1 to 41.9 cm)
- **Weight:** 3.5 to 5.3 ounces (99.2 to 150.3 g)
- **Lifespan:** up to 34 years under human care
- **Conservation Status:** Least Concern

HABITAT & DIET

Able to adapt to a variety of habitats, the Indian ring-necked parakeet feeds on a diet of fruit, seeds, and nuts. In Asia, it can be found from western Pakistan to Burma.

FAMILY & SOCIAL LIFE

These parrots are social birds, forming flocks that fly, communicate, and look for food together.

DID YOU KNOW?

Both male and female birds care for babies, defending their nest and feeding their young.

MOLUCCAN KING PARROT

ALL ABOUT

The Moluccan king parrot stands out with its vibrant red head, green wings, and blue back and tail in males.

- **Length:** 13.8 to 15.7 inches (35.1 to 39.9 cm)
- **Weight:** up to 6 ounces (170.1 g)
- **Lifespan:** 25 to 30 years
- **Conservation Status:** Least Concern

HABITAT & DIET

Found in forests and woodlands primarily of Indonesia, the Moluccan king parrot's diet includes fruit, seeds, nuts, and flowers.

FAMILY & SOCIAL LIFE

These parrots are social but quiet birds, often seen in pairs or small groups. They nest in hollow trees. Chicks are able to live on their own after nine weeks.

FUN FACT

Male Moluccan king parrots use their bright colors to attract mates.

BROWN-HEADED GULL

ALL ABOUT

The brown-headed gull is a migratory bird known for its graceful flight. They are mostly white with a distinct brown head. Their eyes have white rings around them.

- **Length:** 12 to 14 inches (30.5 to 35.6 cm)
- **Weight:** 18.5 to 22.3 ounces (524.5 to 632.2 g)
- **Lifespan:** 21 years
- **Conservation Status:** Least Concern

HABITAT & DIET

Brown-headed gulls live along coastal areas, lakes, and rivers across Eurasia. They eat fish, insects, and crustaceans. They are also known to eat worms from nearby farms and food in garbage dumps.

FUN FACT

Up to several thousand brown-headed gulls can live together in a colony.

FAMILY & SOCIAL LIFE

These gulls nest in colonies and become more social during breeding season.

GREAT KNOT

ALL ABOUT

The great knot is a migratory bird that has a long, straight bill adapted for probing into the mud for food.

- **Length:** 9 to 11 inches (22.9 to 27.9 cm)
- **Weight:** 4.1 to 8.7 ounces (116.2 to 246.6 g)
- **Lifespan:** up to 17 years
- **Conservation Status:** Endangered

HABITAT & DIET

Great knots live primarily on the Siberian tundra but migrate thousands of miles south during the winter months. During the winter, they live in coastal areas and inlets and eat mollusks, crustaceans, and insects.

DID YOU KNOW?

Great knots undertake one of the longest migrations of any bird, traveling from Siberia to Australia and back annually.

FAMILY & SOCIAL LIFE

Great knots often gather in large flocks during migration and breeding seasons.

INDIAN CORMORANT

ALL ABOUT

The Indian cormorant is a slim bird with a long neck and a hooked bill for catching fish underwater. Indian cormorants are divers and often fish as a group.

- **Length:** 24.8 inches (63 cm)
- **Weight:** 1.3 to 1.7 pounds (0.6 to 0.8 kg)
- **Lifespan:** 10 to 15 years
- **Conservation Status:** Least Concern

FUN FACT

Indian cormorants spread their wings to dry after diving.

HABITAT & DIET

Indian cormorants are found mostly along the coasts and wetlands of India, but they can also be found in Bangladesh, Cambodia, and Thailand.

FAMILY & SOCIAL LIFE

These social birds often nest in large colonies. They collectively parent their young. They use twigs to build nests in the forks of trees growing in the water or on islands.

ORIENTAL STORK

ALL ABOUT

Oriental storks have a red bill and are covered in white feathers with black markings. One of the larger species of storks, they are migratory birds known for their graceful flight.

- **Height:** 35.4 to 47.2 inches (89.9 to 119.9 cm)
- **Weight:** 6 to 13 pounds (2.7 to 5.9 kg)
- **Lifespan:** up to 30 years under human care
- **Conservation Status:** Endangered

HABITAT & DIET

They live in wetlands, marshes, and along rivers in Japan, Korea, southeast China, and Siberia. They eat fish, amphibians, and small mammals.

DID YOU KNOW?

Oriental storks are symbols of good luck and fertility in some Asian cultures.

FAMILY & SOCIAL LIFE

Oriental storks are mostly solitary, but they are social during breeding. They build large nests up to 6.6 feet (2 m) in diameter.

RED-CROWNED CRANE

ALL ABOUT

The red-crowned crane is one of the tallest flying birds. It has white plumage with a black band of feathers on the undersides of its wings. It has a small patch of exposed red skin on its head. Long toes help it walk through mud.

- **Length:** 47.2 to 59.1 inches (119.9 to 150.1 cm)
- **Weight:** 15 to 26 pounds (6.8 to 11.8 kg)
- **Lifespan:** 30 years
- **Conservation Status:** Vulnerable

HABITAT & DIET

They live in wetlands, marshes, and grasslands of eastern Asia. They eat plants, grains, insects, and small animals.

FAMILY & SOCIAL LIFE

These cranes live in flocks. They form lifelong partnerships and are known for their courtship dances. Both males and females sit on the nest.

DID YOU KNOW?

Red-crowned cranes are considered symbols of a long life.

RED-LEGGED KITTIWAKE

ALL ABOUT

The red-legged kittiwake has gray-and-white feathers with red legs and feet. This gull is a skilled flyer that predominantly lives on or close to the sea.

- **Length:** 14 to 15.5 inches (35.6 to 39.4 cm)
- **Weight:** 10 to 14 ounces (283.5 to 396.9 g)
- **Lifespan:** 15 to 20 years
- **Conservation Status:** Vulnerable

HABITAT & DIET

These birds are found in the Arctic regions near Russia. In the summer, the birds live on and around rocky cliffs. In the winter, they migrate to the sea. Their regular diet includes fish, squid, and crustaceans.

FUN FACT

Red-legged kittiwakes are known for their loud, lively calls during the breeding season.

FAMILY & SOCIAL LIFE

Red-legged kittiwakes live and nest together in colonies on cliff slopes. Both parents watch after the chicks, feeding them regurgitated food.

ASIAN GREEN BEE-EATER

ALL ABOUT

Asian green bee-eaters are brightly colored birds with a long, curved bill. They have black stripes that give them a mask-like appearance. Green bee-eaters can catch insects with their wings and are good at hunting in the air.

FUN FACT

Green bee-eaters hit insects against rocks to remove dirt before eating them.

- **Length:** 6 to 7 inches (15.2 to 17.8 cm)
- **Weight:** 0.5 to 0.7 ounces (14.2 to 19.8 g)
- **Lifespan:** 12 to 18 years
- **Conservation Status:** Least Concern

HABITAT & DIET

Ranging across southern Asia, these birds stay near open areas and forests with scattered trees and bushes. Their diet includes bees, wasps, and other flying insects.

FAMILY & SOCIAL LIFE

They nest together in groups of up to 300 birds and swarm together to attack insects.

BLACK-WINGED MYNA

ALL ABOUT

Also called a black-winged starling, the black-winged myna has glossy black feathers with white patches on its wings. There are no feathers around its eyes, which are surrounded by a bright-yellow patch of skin.

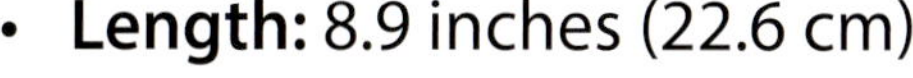

- **Length:** 8.9 inches (22.6 cm)
- **Weight:** 3.8 to 6 ounces (107.7 to 170.1 g)
- **Lifespan:** 10 to 15 years
- **Conservation Status:** Endangered

HABITAT & DIET

Black-winged mynas live in forests, woodlands, and urban areas in Indonesia. They eat fruit, insects, and small vertebrates.

FUN FACT

Black-winged mynas have become endangered in part due to being illegally poached and sold as caged birds.

FAMILY & SOCIAL LIFE

Black-winged mynas are social birds known for their loud calls and playful behavior. They often live in large flocks. They are monogamous when mating.

Brown-eared bulbul

BULBULS

ALL ABOUT

Bulbuls are a family of more than 100 bird species, known for their songs and wide array of plumage colors. They are often seen hopping and flitting between branches in trees. They are usually heard before they are seen.

- **Length:** 5.5 to 11 inches (14 to 27.9 cm)
- **Weight:** 1 to 3.3 ounces (28.3 to 93.6 g)
- **Lifespan:** up to 11 years
- **Conservation Status:** Least Concern to Critically Endangered

HABITAT & DIET

Bulbuls live in a variety of habitats throughout Asia, including forests, gardens, and shrublands. They eat fruit and small insects and drink nectar.

FAMILY & SOCIAL LIFE

They are social birds that often form small groups or pairs. They may also be seen with other bird species.

BROWN-EARED BULBUL

The brown-eared bulbul may be different colors depending on where it lives.

RED-WHISKERED BULBUL

The red-whiskered bulbul is named for the bright patches of red underneath its eyes.

YELLOW-BROWED BULBUL

Yellow-browed bulbuls lay only two or three eggs per year. They feed their chicks berries and soft insects after hatching.

FUN FACT

Some bulbuls have specialized adaptations, such as curved bills for taking nectar from flowers.

Red-whiskered bulbul

Yellow-browed bulbul

FIRE-TAILED MYZORNIS

ALL ABOUT

A fire-tailed myzornis is a compact bird with bright red plumage on its tail, contrasting with its green-and-yellow body. A fire-tailed myzornis is a shy bird often found hiding in dense vegetation and bamboo thickets.

- **Length:** 4 to 5 inches (10.2 to 12.7 cm)
- **Weight:** 0.4 to 0.5 ounces (11.3 to 14.2 g)
- **Lifespan:** unknown
- **Conservation Status:** Least Concern

HABITAT & DIET

They live in mountain forests and scrublands at the foot of the Himalayas. They eat insects, spiders, berries, and flower nectar.

DID YOU KNOW?

The fire-tailed myzornis is known for its acrobatic flight and graceful movements in dense vegetation.

FAMILY & SOCIAL LIFE

Fire-tailed myzornis are often seen in pairs or small groups and may join mixed-species flocks for hunting.

PALLAS'S LEAF-WARBLER

ALL ABOUT

Pallas's leaf-warblers are olive-green migratory birds. They are busy and restless birds, making fast and energetic movements while constantly hunting.

- **Length:** 3 to 4 inches (7.6 to 10.2 cm)
- **Weight:** 0.2 to 0.3 ounces (5.7 to 8.5 g)
- **Lifespan:** unknown
- **Conservation Status:** Least Concern

FUN FACT

These busy birds often hover in midair to catch insects.

HABITAT & DIET

They live in evergreen trees in mountain forests and woodlands of eastern Asia. During breeding season, they migrate north to Siberia. They often pick insects and berries from the trees for eating.

FAMILY & SOCIAL LIFE

These warblers gather in similar areas and sometimes are seen with other bird species while hunting. Nests are built along tree trunks and in bushes. Both parents feed and care for hatched babies.

BAR-HEADED GOOSE

ALL ABOUT

Bar-headed geese are one of the world's highest-flying birds, migrating over the Himalayas. They can be identified by two bars of dark feathers that wrap around the back of their head.

- **Length:** 27 to 30 inches (68.6 to 76.2 cm)
- **Weight:** 4 to 6 pounds (1.8 to 2.7 kg)
- **Lifespan:** 20 years
- **Conservation Status:** Least Concern

HABITAT & DIET

They prefer to live near freshwater lakes and marshes of India during the winter. In the summer, they live in mountain grasslands of central Asia. They mainly eat grasses, grains, and occasionally insects and mollusks.

FAMILY & SOCIAL LIFE

They travel in large flocks in a V formation during migration and nest together in colonies.

DID YOU KNOW?

Bar-headed geese have strong wing muscles and lungs, which help them fly long distances.

MANDARIN DUCK

ALL ABOUT

The male mandarin duck is known for its bold coloring, elaborate plumage, and red bill. Females tend to be mostly brown with a gray head. Both males and females are known to be shy birds.

- **Length:** 16 to 20 inches (40.6 to 50.8 cm)
- **Weight:** 15.1 to 24.4 ounces (428.1 to 691.7 g)
- **Lifespan:** 3 to 12 years
- **Conservation Status:** Least Concern

HABITAT & DIET

Mandarin ducks are found near ponds, rivers, and forests in China, Japan, Korea, and parts of Russia. They hunt on land and in the water. Their diet includes insects, fish, and worms.

FUN FACT

Mandarin ducks are symbols of love in Chinese culture and are often shown in traditional art.

FAMILY & SOCIAL LIFE

Mandarin ducks form monogamous pairs during breeding season and stay in flocks of more than 60 birds.

SWAN GOOSE

ALL ABOUT

Swan geese are geese with features similar to swans. They have a long neck and a long black bill.

- **Length:** 30 to 36 inches (76.2 to 91.4 cm)
- **Weight:** 4 to 8 pounds (1.8 to 3.6 kg)
- **Lifespan:** 20 years under human care
- **Conservation Status:** Endangered

HABITAT & DIET

Swan geese live around lakes, marshes, and grasslands in northeastern China and Russia. They hunt in the morning and evening, eating mostly grasses, aquatic plants, and grains.

FUN FACT

The back side of the swan goose's neck is dark brown, and the front is a light cream color.

FAMILY & SOCIAL LIFE

Swan geese are social birds often found in small flocks near water bodies. They form monogamous pairs during breeding and may migrate with birds from other species.

WHOOPER SWAN

ALL ABOUT

The whooper swan is a large swan with white plumage, a long neck, and a yellow bill. These birds are strong and graceful swimmers and are known for their bugle-like call.

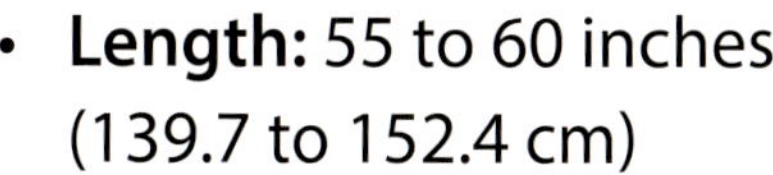

- **Length:** 55 to 60 inches (139.7 to 152.4 cm)
- **Weight:** 15 to 25 pounds (6.8 to 11.3 kg)
- **Lifespan:** 20 to 25 years
- **Conservation Status:** Least Concern

HABITAT & DIET

They are found in freshwater lakes, ponds, and marshes of northern Asia and Siberia. Their diet includes aquatic plants, grains, worms, and mollusks. They dip their beak into water to hunt.

FAMILY & SOCIAL LIFE

These swans spend their days swimming and eating water plants. They live in both small and larger flocks.

FUN FACT

Baby whooper swans are called cygnets.

GREAT BUSTARD

ALL ABOUT

Great bustards migrate more than 2,000 miles (3,218.7 km) and can fly at speeds of up to 50 miles per hour (80.5 kmh).

- **Length:** 35 to 47 inches (88.9 to 119.4 cm)
- **Weight:** 10 to 30 pounds (4.5 to 13.6 kg)
- **Lifespan:** 10 to 15 years
- **Conservation Status:** Endangered

HABITAT & DIET

Great bustards live in grasslands and fields of central Asia, eating plants, insects, and small vertebrates.

FAMILY & SOCIAL LIFE

These birds are mostly solitary with established territories during breeding.

FUN FACT

A great bustard's call can be heard miles away.

IBIS

ALL ABOUT

Ibises have long, curved bills and long, thin legs. They sometimes have bare skin on their face and throat. Ibises wade into shallow water in groups to dig for food.

- **Length:** 20 to 30 inches (50.8 to 76.2 cm)
- **Weight:** up to 10 pounds (4.5 kg)
- **Lifespan:** up to 20 years
- **Conservation Status:** Least Concern to Endangered

HABITAT & DIET

Ibises live in wetlands, swamps, marshes, and coastal areas in warm regions across Asia. They eat insects, crustaceans, and small fish.

FUN FACT

Some ibis species flash their wings as a show of dominance in courtship.

FAMILY & SOCIAL LIFE

Many ibis species form large colonies for breeding, nesting, and raising their young. Both parents participate in incubating the eggs and caring for the chicks.

LESSER BIRD-OF-PARADISE

ALL ABOUT

Lesser birds-of-paradise are brightly colored with long tail feathers and a yellow crown. Males also have a pair of wire-like tail plumes.

- **Length:** 10 to 12 inches (25.4 to 30.5 cm)
- **Weight:** 1 to 2.1 ounces (28.3 to 59.5 g)
- **Lifespan:** unknown
- **Conservation Status:** Least Concern

HABITAT & DIET

They live in trees in rainforests and lowland forests of New Guinea. They eat fruit, insects, and small vertebrates.

FAMILY & SOCIAL LIFE

Females lay one or two pink eggs and care for the chicks until they leave the nest at about three weeks.

FUN FACT

Male lesser birds-of-paradise put on an elaborate dance and show off their feathers to attract female mates.

PEACOCK

ALL ABOUT

Peacocks, sometimes called Indian peafowl, are known for their elaborate plumage, especially the long tail feathers of males. They live on the ground but are skilled climbers that roost in trees.

- **Length:** 2.8 to 7 feet (0.9 to 2.1 m)
- **Weight:** 8 to 13 pounds (3.6 to 5.9 kg)
- **Lifespan:** 20 to 25 years
- **Conservation Status:** Least Concern

HABITAT & DIET

Peacocks live in forests, grasslands, and fields of India, Sri Lanka, and other parts of southern Asia. They eat seeds, plants, insects, and small animals.

FAMILY & SOCIAL LIFE

Peacocks build shallow ground nests, usually hidden in vegetation for protection. The chicks, called peachicks, can follow their mother shortly after hatching.

DID YOU KNOW?

The vibrant tail feathers of male peacocks, known as a train, can reach up to 5 feet (1.5 m) long and are used in courtship displays and territorial defense.

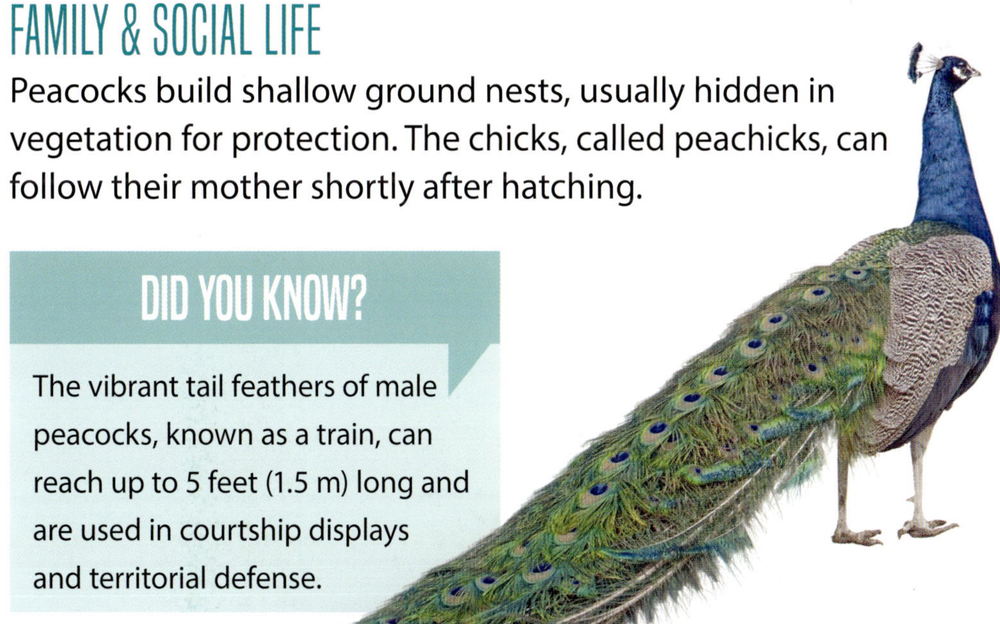

KINGFISHER

- **About:** Kingfishers are known for their hunting skills, diving into the water to catch fish with precision.
- **Habitat:** forests, near rivers
- **Conservation Status:** Least Concern

Kingfisher

PALESTINE SUNBIRD

- **About:** Palestine sunbirds have a metallic sheen to their feathers. These birds are found in the Middle East.
- **Habitat:** woodlands and orchards
- **Conservation Status:** Least Concern

Palestine sunbird

RUFOUS-HEADED ROBIN

- **About:** Rufous-headed robins are known for their mating songs.
- **Habitat:** forests
- **Conservation Status:** Endangered

Rufous-headed robin

Siberian jay

SIBERIAN JAY

- **About:** Siberian jays are known for their intelligence and ability to store food for winter.
- **Habitat:** forests
- **Conservation Status:** Least Concern

YEMEN LINNET

- **About:** Yemen linnets are brightly colored and sing cheerful songs.
- **Habitat:** forests, river valleys
- **Conservation Status:** Least Concern

Yemen linnet

FISH AND CRUSTACEANS

Giant Mekong catfish

Fish are animals that live in the water. Some live in fresh water, such as rivers and lakes, whereas others live in saltwater oceans and seas. Most fish have gills that help them breathe. There are two different types of fish. Bony fish have skeletons made of bone, whereas cartilaginous fish have skeletons made of cartilage. Most fish are bony. Sharks and rays are cartilaginous.

Fiddler crab

Crustaceans are invertebrates. They don't have a backbone. Most crustaceans live in water, and they can be found around the world.

Fish and crustaceans are diverse in size, shape, color, and behavior. They play crucial roles in their ecosystems and serve as food sources for humans as well as one another.

Koi carp

ASIAN CARP

ALL ABOUT

Asian carp can be considered invasive because they grow fast and reproduce often.

- **Length:** 4 feet (1.2 m)
- **Weight:** 100 pounds (45.4 kg)
- **Lifespan:** 15 to 20 years
- **Conservation Status:** Near Threatened

HABITAT & DIET

Asian carp live in freshwater rivers and lakes in China and parts of Russia. They eat plankton, algae, and various floating matter.

DURBAN DANCING SHRIMP

ALL ABOUT

These small crustaceans dart and dance among coral reefs and rocky crevices.

- **Length:** up to 1.6 inches (4.1 cm)
- **Weight:** less than 1 ounce (28.4 g)
- **Lifespan:** 1 to 2 years
- **Conservation Status:** Not Assessed

HABITAT & DIET

Found in tropical waters of the western Indian Ocean, they feed on plankton.

FIDDLER CRAB

ALL ABOUT

Fiddler crabs have one oversized claw (usually on males) that they use for communication, feeding, and defense.

- **Length:** 2 inches (5 cm)
- **Weight:** not enough data
- **Lifespan:** 1 to 2 years
- **Conservation Status:** Not Assessed

FUN FACT

One enlarged claw makes the male fiddler crab look like it's holding a violin.

HABITAT & DIET

They are burrowing crustaceans that live across the coasts of eastern Asia. They eat the matter they find in the mud and sand.

FAMILY & SOCIAL LIFE

They form social colonies, with males using their large claws in courtship displays.

KOI CARP

ALL ABOUT

Koi carp are known for their vibrant colors and patterns. They are often kept in ponds and aquariums.

- **Length:** 12 to 36 inches (30.5 to 91.4 cm)
- **Weight:** 35 pounds (15.9 kg)
- **Lifespan:** 40 years
- **Conservation Status:** Not Assessed

HABITAT & DIET

Koi carp are native to freshwater habitats around the Aral, Caspian, and Black Seas. They feed on plants and insects.

FAMILY & SOCIAL LIFE

They are social fish that stay in well-structured groups.

DID YOU KNOW?

Koi were first domesticated in China, as far back as the fourth century.

MANTIS SHRIMP

ALL ABOUT

Mantis shrimp have powerful claws they use to quickly and forcefully punch prey. There are more than 400 species of this aggressive predator.

- **Length:** 4 to 15 inches (10.2 to 38.1 cm)
- **Weight:** 0.4 to 3.2 ounces (11.3 to 90.7 g)
- **Lifespan:** 5 to 7 years
- **Conservation Status:** Not Assessed

FUN FACT

Mantis shrimp have highly developed visual skills. They can detect not only a wide range of colors but also cancer.

HABITAT & DIET

They are found in tropical and subtropical waters of the Indian and Pacific Oceans, often hiding in burrows or rocky crevices. They feed on fish, worms, snails, and other mollusks.

FAMILY & SOCIAL LIFE

They are generally solitary and territorial. They fiercely protect their home territory.

MUDSKIPPER

ALL ABOUT

Mudskippers are amphibious fish that can breathe air and walk using their fins. They have bulging eyes and are sometimes called gobies.

- **Length:** 4 to 12 inches (10.2 to 30.5 cm)
- **Weight:** 1.8 ounces (51 g)
- **Lifespan:** 2 to 4 years
- **Conservation Status:** Least Concern

HABITAT & DIET

They are found in coastal areas, mangrove swamps, and tidal flats of southern Asia, where they move between land and water. Mudskippers eat insects, shellfish, and other small fish.

FUN FACT

Male mudskippers get female attention by jumping high above the mud.

FAMILY & SOCIAL LIFE

Mudskippers are often seen in small groups or pairs. They are protective of their burrows, where they lay eggs.

PACIFIC BLUEFIN TUNA

ALL ABOUT

Pacific bluefin tuna are large fish known for their speed and endurance. They are powerful swimmers found in open oceans, often traveling long distances in search of food.

- **Length:** up to 9.8 feet (3 m)
- **Weight:** 300 to 990 pounds (136.1 to 449.1 kg)
- **Lifespan:** 15 to 26 years
- **Conservation Status:** Near Threatened

HABITAT & DIET

These tuna feed on small fish, squid, and shellfish. They are found along the eastern Asian coast.

FAMILY & SOCIAL LIFE

Spawning happens in the Sea of Japan and, within a year, the tuna travels more than 5,000 miles (8,046.7 km) to spend years eating and growing along the North American coastline.

SPIDER CRAB

ALL ABOUT

Spider crabs are large with long, spindly legs and a rounded body. They live at the bottom of the ocean where they search for food.

- **Length:** up to 13.1 feet (4 m)
- **Weight:** 35.3 to 44.1 pounds (16 to 20 kg)
- **Lifespan:** 50 to 100 years
- **Conservation Status:** Not Assessed

HABITAT & DIET

The largest spider crabs are found in Japan and feed on debris, worms, seaweed, and algae. They use their claws to catch and crush their food.

FAMILY & SOCIAL LIFE

They often gather together to breed in shallow waters. Hatched larvae float on the surface until they develop into crabs.

The spider crab's body and legs are covered with fine hairs and bumps, which are often covered in algae and ocean waste.

TIGER TAIL SEAHORSE

ALL ABOUT

Tiger tail seahorses have a long, slender body with a curved tail used for grasping seagrasses or corals. These seahorses use camouflage to avoid predators.

- **Length:** 4.7 to 6.3 inches (11.9 to 16 cm)
- **Weight:** not enough data
- **Lifespan:** 3 to 5 years
- **Conservation Status:** Vulnerable

FUN FACT

Baby seahorses are called fry.

HABITAT & DIET

Tiger tail seahorses live in coral reefs and seagrass areas in Southeast Asia. They eat small shellfish and plankton, sucking prey into their tube-shaped mouth.

FAMILY & SOCIAL LIFE

They are generally solitary and territorial, with males carrying eggs in a pouch until they hatch. Seahorses are one of the few species where males give birth to offspring.

ADDITIONAL FISH AND CRUSTACEANS

Chinese mitten crab

CHINESE MITTEN CRAB

- **About:** Chinese mitten crabs have hairy claws that resemble mittens, which they use for digging burrows and handling food.
- **Habitat:** brackish water
- **Conservation Status:** Not Assessed

HORNED GHOST CRAB

- **About:** Horned ghost crabs have excellent eyesight. They quickly retreat into their burrows at the slightest sign of danger.
- **Habitat:** ocean coastlines
- **Conservation Status:** Not Assessed

Horned ghost crab

INDO-PACIFIC SERGEANT

- **About:** Indo-Pacific sergeants primarily eat algae and small crustaceans.
- **Habitat:** coral reefs
- **Conservation Status:** Least Concern

Indo-Pacific sergeant

SPOTTED EAGLE RAY

- **About:** Spotted eagle rays have whip-like tails with venomous spines.
- **Habitat:** tropical waters
- **Conservation Status:** Vulnerable

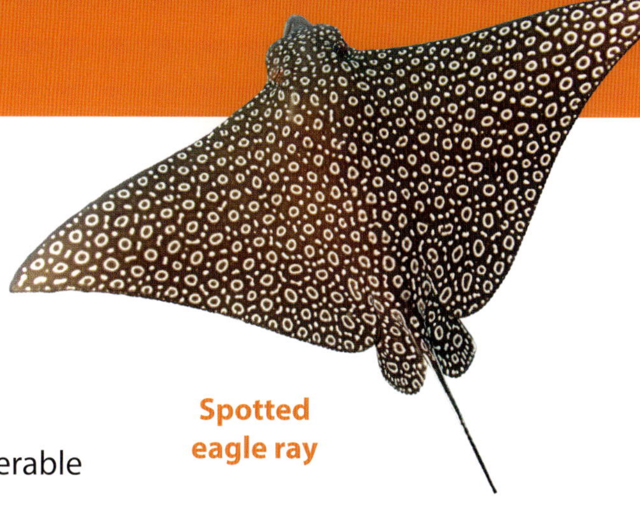

Spotted eagle ray

Yellowfin surgeonfish

YELLOWFIN SURGEONFISH

- **About:** Yellowfin surgeonfish are social fish, communicating through body language and color changes, especially during feeding and breeding.
- **Habitat:** reefs
- **Conservation Status:** Least Concern

ZANDER

- **About:** Zander are known as aggressive fighters.
- **Habitat:** freshwater and brackish habitats
- **Conservation Status:** Least Concern

Zander

AMPHIBIANS

Amphibians are vertebrates that can live both in the water and on land. Most amphibians need to stay moist. They often breathe through their skin. Amphibians start life as eggs laid in water. When they hatch, the larvae stay in the water until they develop into their adult forms. Then they can leave the water and start life on land.

Amphibians are cold-blooded. When they get too cold, they become less active. Many amphibians produce bad-tasting poison, which protects them from predators.

Asian common toad

Chinese giant salamander

Amphibians in Asia include frogs, toads, salamanders, and newts. They range in size from the Japanese giant salamander, which can reach over 5 feet (1.5 m) in length, to the Borneo pygmy frog, which is less than a half inch (1.3 cm) long. Amphibians help lower the mosquito populations, which sometimes cause disease. They also serve as food for larger animal species.

Japanese fire-bellied newt

ASIAN COMMON TOAD

ALL ABOUT

The Asian common toad, also known as the Asian spiny toad, has warty skin with short spines. They range in color, but most are yellowish brown with dark spots.

- **Length:** 2 to 4 inches (5.1 to 10.2 cm)
- **Weight:** 0.7 to 2.8 ounces (19.8 to 79.4 g)
- **Lifespan:** 4 years
- **Conservation Status:** Least Concern

HABITAT & DIET

Asian common toads tend to live near water in forests, grasslands, or agricultural areas of southern China, India, and Southeast Asia. They are nocturnal and eat mostly insects.

FAMILY & SOCIAL LIFE

They gather in groups near water for mating but mostly live on their own. Males compete for female attention.

FUN FACT

Asian common toads have large glands behind their eyes that release toxins.

BEDDOME'S CAECILIAN

ALL ABOUT

The Beddome's caecilian is a worm-like amphibian with narrow eyes and a body that is made for burrowing in the earth.

- **Length:** 6.7 to 10.8 inches (17 to 27.4 cm)
- **Weight:** 2.2 pounds (1 kg)
- **Lifespan:** 10 to 15 years
- **Conservation Status:** Least Concern

HABITAT & DIET

Beddome's caecilians are found in moist soil, leaf litter, and rotting logs in southern India. They eat earthworms, insect larvae, and small beetles and other bugs.

DID YOU KNOW?

Beddome's caecilians spend most of their life underground.

FAMILY & SOCIAL LIFE

They stay aboveground except during rainy periods and during breeding season. Females take care of the nest of eggs but leave before they hatch.

CHINESE GIANT SALAMANDER

ALL ABOUT

The Chinese giant salamander is the world's largest amphibian. It has a flat body and speckled skin, providing camouflage against rocky river bottoms. This salamander lives in the water, but it doesn't have gills. Instead, it absorbs oxygen through its skin.

- **Length:** 3.7 to 6 feet (1.1 to 1.8 m)
- **Weight:** up to 110.2 pounds (50 kg)
- **Lifespan:** 60 years under human care
- **Conservation Status:** Critically Endangered

HABITAT & DIET

Chinese giant salamanders live in mountain rivers and streams of central China. They feed on fish, shellfish, other amphibians, and small mammals.

FAMILY & SOCIAL LIFE

Females lay up to 500 eggs in an underwater burrow. The eggs are then fertilized and protected by males.

FUN FACT

Chinese giant salamanders are considered living fossils, with ancestors dating back over 170 million years.

COMMON TREE FROG

ALL ABOUT

Common tree frogs are differentiated from toads by their sticky toe pads that help them climb and cling to leaves. They live in trees and shrubs near water bodies.

- **Length:** 1.5 to 2 inches (3.8 to 5.1 cm)
- **Weight:** not enough data
- **Lifespan:** 2 to 5 years
- **Conservation Status:** Least Concern

FUN FACT

Common tree frogs can change color to match their surroundings.

HABITAT & DIET

Common tree frogs live in forests, gardens, and wetlands of southern Asia. At night, they hunt spiders and insects, including beetles.

FAMILY & SOCIAL LIFE

Females lay 100 to 400 eggs in a foamy nest in the water. The tadpoles grow on the water's surface before developing their limbs and moving to the trees.

JAPANESE FIRE-BELLIED NEWT

ALL ABOUT

Japanese fire-bellied newts are orange with black markings. These bright colors warn predators that the newts' skin contains harmful toxins.

- **Length:** 3 to 5 inches (7.6 to 12.7 cm)
- **Weight:** not enough data
- **Lifespan:** 10 to 15 years under human care
- **Conservation Status:** Near Threatened

HABITAT & DIET

Japanese fire-bellied newts are found in ponds, streams, and wetlands of Japan. They eat small water insects, worms, and tadpoles. They use their sticky tongues to catch prey.

FAMILY & SOCIAL LIFE

Females lay eggs on materials that are underwater. The tadpoles hatch about three weeks later.

FUN FACT

Female Japanese fire-bellied newts are larger than males.

JAPANESE GIANT SALAMANDER

ALL ABOUT

The Japanese giant salamander is the second-largest amphibian in the world. Like the Chinese giant salamander, it breathes through its skin. It does have a single lung, which helps to control buoyancy in the water.

- **Length:** 3 to 5 feet (0.9 to 1.5 m)
- **Weight:** 25 to 55 pounds (11.3 to 24.9 kg)
- **Lifespan:** 30 to 50 years
- **Conservation Status:** Vulnerable

HABITAT & DIET

The Japanese giant salamander is found in fast-running streams in the mountain regions of central Japan. They eat fish, small animals, and other amphibians.

FUN FACT

Japanese giant salamanders can regenerate their skin and bones.

FAMILY & SOCIAL LIFE

During breeding season, males guard nests, and females lay eggs under rocks or in burrows.

LURISTAN NEWT

ALL ABOUT

Luristan newts are small with patches of black, white, and orange. An orange stripe runs along their back.

- **Length:** 3.9 to 5.5 inches (9.9 to 14 cm)
- **Weight:** not enough data
- **Lifespan:** 14 years
- **Conservation Status:** Vulnerable

HABITAT & DIET

Luristan newts live in mountain streams and springs in a small area of Iran. They eat worms, mollusks, small fish, and larvae.

FAMILY & SOCIAL LIFE

During mating season, males dance to attract females. Females produce about 60 eggs, which they lay on rocks or in vegetation.

WALLACE'S FLYING FROG

ALL ABOUT

Wallace's flying frogs have webbed feet and toes, allowing these frogs to glide from tree to tree.

- **Length:** up to 4 inches (10.2 cm)
- **Weight:** 1 ounce (28.3 g)
- **Lifespan:** 5 to 8 years
- **Conservation Status:** Least Concern

HABITAT & DIET

They live in tropical rainforests of Southeast Asia. They eat insects such as ants, termites, and beetles.

FAMILY & SOCIAL LIFE

Females lay eggs in a foam nest. Tadpoles develop in the water.

FUN FACT

Wallace's flying frogs can glide up to 50 feet (15.2 m) in a single leap.

ADDITIONAL AMPHIBIANS

DYBOWSKI'S FROG

- **About:** The Dybowski's frog has a loud and distinctive call during mating season.
- **Habitat:** wooded areas
- **Conservation Status:** Near Threatened

Dybowski's frog

Eastern spadefoot toad

EASTERN SPADEFOOT TOAD

- **About:** Eastern spadefoot toads have spade-like projections on their hind feet used for burrowing.
- **Habitat:** loose, sandy soil
- **Conservation Status:** Least Concern

GLIDING FROG

- **About:** Gliding frogs have adapted skin flaps that help them glide between trees.
- **Habitat:** rainforests
- **Conservation Status:** Least Concern

Gliding frog

HARLEQUIN TREE FROG

- **About:** Harlequin tree frogs can be identified by their yellow sides with black spots.
- **Habitat:** tropical forests
- **Conservation Status:** Least Concern

Harlequin tree frog

Leaf litter toad

LEAF LITTER TOAD

- **About:** Leaf litter toads camouflage by looking like dead leaves.
- **Habitat:** forest floor
- **Conservation Status:** Varies by species

PERSIAN BROOK SALAMANDER

- **About:** Persian brook salamanders live in caves in a small area of Iran.
- **Habitat:** rivers and springs
- **Conservation Status:** Vulnerable

Persian brook salamander

INSECTS AND ARACHNIDS

There are more insects than any other type of animal on Earth. More than one million species of insects have been discovered. Insects are a type of arthropod. They have six legs and a segmented body. They don't have skeletons. Instead, they have exoskeletons, which are on the outside of their bodies. Insects live in every habitat all over the world.

Apollo butterfly

Asian long-horned beetle

Arachnids are also arthropods. Like insects, they have exoskeletons, but they have eight legs and live only on land. Spiders and scorpions are examples of arachnids. Most arachnids sit and wait for prey before ambushing it. Others, such as ticks, are parasites. A very small number of arachnids eat vegetation.

Camel spider

APOLLO BUTTERFLY

ALL ABOUT

The large apollo butterfly has mostly white wings with black stripes and dots. Two red dots are on each hind wing.

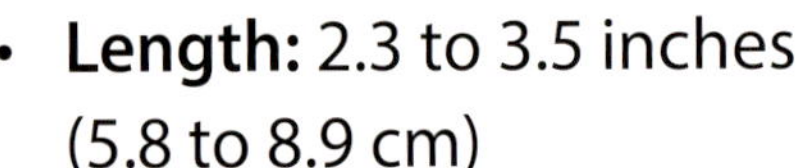

- **Length:** 2.3 to 3.5 inches (5.8 to 8.9 cm)
- **Weight:** not enough data
- **Lifespan:** up to 2 weeks
- **Conservation Status:** Least Concern

HABITAT & DIET

Because these butterflies feed mostly on nectar, they prefer mountain meadows and grasslands of central Asia. As caterpillars, they eat a lot of leaves and vegetation.

FUN FACT

The red dots on an apollo butterfly can fade to orange after being in the sunlight.

FAMILY & SOCIAL LIFE

Unlike most butterfly species that make a chrysalis, the apollo makes a cocoon-like web. There, the caterpillar pupates into a butterfly. Male butterflies have territories that they defend against others.

ASIAN GIANT HORNET

ALL ABOUT

This orange-and-black hornet is the world's largest.

- **Length:** up to 2 inches (5.1 cm)
- **Weight:** not enough data
- **Lifespan:** up to 1 year
- **Conservation Status:** Not Assessed

HABITAT & DIET

Found in forests and low mountain areas of southern and eastern Asia, these hornets aggressively attack and eat their prey, mostly other insects.

ASIAN LONG-HORNED BEETLE

ALL ABOUT

These black-and-white beetles are invasive and destructive to trees.

- **Length:** 1.5 inches (3.8 cm)
- **Weight:** not enough data
- **Lifespan:** 50 to 66 days
- **Conservation Status:** Not Assessed

HABITAT & DIET

Originally native to forests in eastern China and Korea, these beetles bore into trees to deposit eggs. Adult beetles feed on twigs and leaves.

ATLAS MOTH

ALL ABOUT

The atlas moth is one of the largest moths in the world. Its coloring and patterning help it camouflage in its forest habitat.

- **Wingspan:** up to 12 inches (30.5 cm)
- **Weight:** not enough data
- **Lifespan:** up to 2 weeks as an adult
- **Conservation Status:** Not Assessed

DID YOU KNOW?

Atlas moths have wing patterns that resemble snake heads, which can deter predators.

HABITAT & DIET

Atlas moths are native to China, India, and Southeast Asia. Caterpillars eat the leaves of tropical fruit trees. However, adult moths do not eat, as they don't have fully formed mouths.

FAMILY & SOCIAL LIFE

The moths rest on trees and only move at night, saving their energy for reproduction. After mating, the female lays about 150 eggs and then dies.

BHUTAN GLORY

ALL ABOUT

Bhutan glory butterflies are black with white-and-red markings. They have wide top wings and flowing rear wings.

- **Wingspan:** 3.5 to 4.3 inches (8.9 to 10.9 cm)
- **Weight:** not enough data
- **Lifespan:** 179 days
- **Conservation Status:** Least Concern

HABITAT & DIET

Bhutan glory butterflies live in mountain areas near Bhutan, Southeast Asia, and India. They prefer to stay near the tops of trees. Their diet consists primarily of nectar.

FUN FACT

The Bhutan glory adult has a long life for a butterfly—about 180 days. Most adult butterflies live only 7 to 10 days.

FAMILY & SOCIAL LIFE

The life cycle of the Bhutan glory was a mystery until 2019, when scientists learned the larvae go through eight stages before emerging as a butterfly.

CAMEL SPIDER

ALL ABOUT

Resembling both a spider and a scorpion, the camel spider has a hairy face and legs and large pincher-like jaws. It runs fast and is an aggressive hunter.

- **Length:** up to 6 inches (15.2 cm)
- **Weight:** 1 to 2 ounces (28.3 to 56.7 g)
- **Lifespan:** 1 to 2 years
- **Conservation Status:** Not Assessed

HABITAT & DIET

Found in Asia's deserts, the camel spider eats insects, small reptiles, and rodents.

FAMILY & SOCIAL LIFE

After mating, the female digs an underground burrow and lays 50 to 200 eggs. The mother may protect her babies from predators. The young can go through several stages before maturing.

FUN FACT

Camel spiders are a type of arachnid called Solifugae, which are neither spiders nor scorpions.

DRAGONFLY

ALL ABOUT

There are around 3,000 species of dragonflies. They are known for their flying skills and aggressive hunting abilities.

- **Wingspan:** 2 to 5 inches (5.1 to 12.7 cm)
- **Weight:** 0.1 to 0.2 ounces (2.8 to 5.7 g)
- **Lifespan:** 7 to 56 days
- **Conservation Status:** Least Concern

HABITAT & DIET

Dragonflies live near freshwater habitats such as ponds and rivers across Asia. They eat mostly other flying insects, like mosquitoes. They are aerial predators, only eating prey that they can catch midair.

FUN FACT

Dragonflies have been around for millions of years.

FAMILY & SOCIAL LIFE

Males and females form a wheel shape as they mate. The female lays eggs in the water, where they hatch. Larvae live in the water and don't become adults for up to two years.

INDIAN FLOWER MANTIS

ALL ABOUT

The small Indian flower mantis is slow-moving but active. This mostly white insect has brightly colored wings. It is an ambush predator that waits for prey before attacking.

- **Length:** up to 2 inches (5.1 cm)
- **Weight:** not enough data
- **Lifespan:** 1 to 2 years
- **Conservation Status:** Not Assessed

FUN FACT

The brightly colored wings of an Indian flower mantis mimic flowers, which attract prey.

HABITAT & DIET

These insects are native to the tropical rainforests of Asia. They live on fruit flies and other small insects.

FAMILY & SOCIAL LIFE

After mating, a female mantis may lay her eggs in a foamy structure called an ootheca until they hatch. She may also eat the head of the male after breeding.

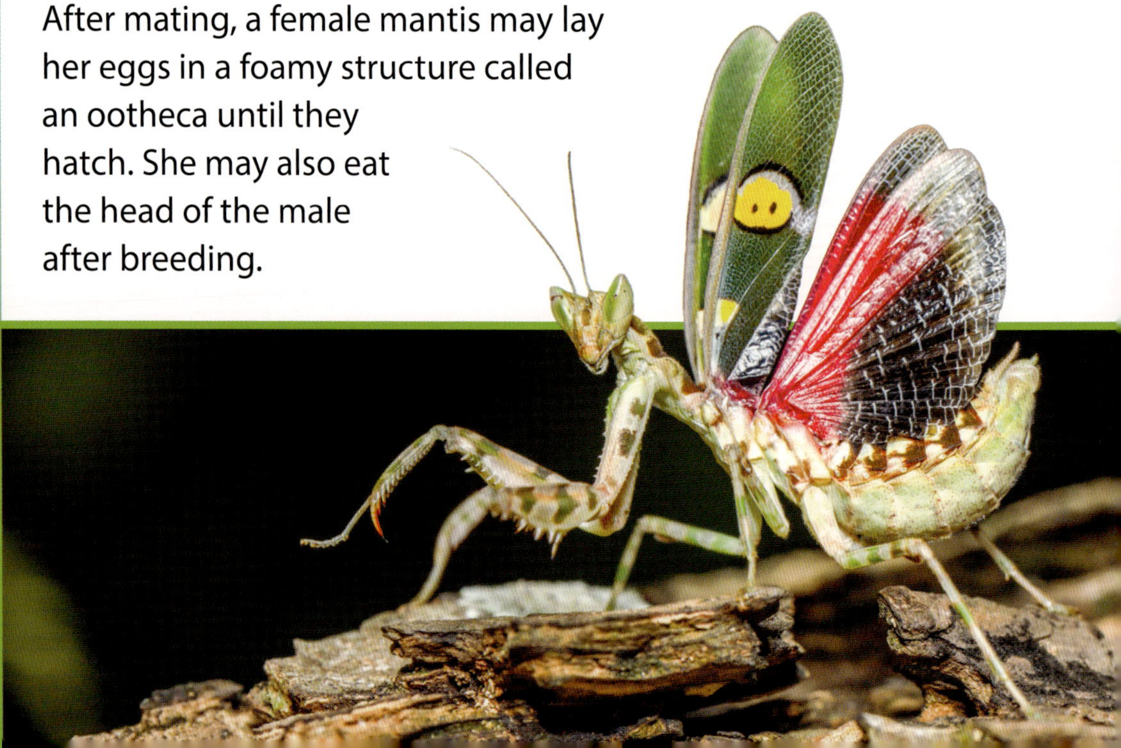

JAPANESE CARPENTER ANT

ALL ABOUT

The large Japanese carpenter ant has strong jaws that help it chew through wood and build nests.

- **Length:** 0.7 inches (1.8 cm)
- **Weight:** not enough data
- **Lifespan:** varies
- **Conservation Status:** Not Assessed

HABITAT & DIET

Native to eastern Asia, these ants live underground but spend much of their time in decaying wood and logs. Their diet consists of other insects such as aphids and flies.

FAMILY & SOCIAL LIFE

This black ant lives in nests of several hundred workers, or soldiers, and a single queen. They each have a task in the social structure, including finding food and caring for young.

FUN FACT

Japanese carpenter ants communicate with one another through their antennae.

RHINOCEROS BEETLE

ALL ABOUT

Rhinoceros beetles are the largest beetles in the world. They are recognized by the horns on the male's head. These horns are used for fighting over females as well as for territory.

- **Length:** 2 to 7 inches (5.1 to 17.8 cm)
- **Weight:** 0.3 to 0.4 ounces (8.5 to 11.3 g)
- **Lifespan:** up to 1 year
- **Conservation Status:** Not Assessed

HABITAT & DIET

These flying beetles live in rainforests and grasslands across much of Asia. As herbivores, they eat plants, sap, nectar, and rotting wood.

FAMILY & SOCIAL LIFE

Eggs are laid in decaying wood and then develop into grubs. After about a year, they transform into beetles.

FUN FACT

Rhinoceros beetles are among the strongest insects, capable of lifting objects 100 times their body weight.

SIGNATURE SPIDER

ALL ABOUT

The signature spider gets its name by building a web of zigzag patterns that resemble a signature. These webs help them to catch prey.

- **Length:** up to 0.5 inches (1.3 cm)
- **Weight:** not enough data
- **Lifespan:** 1 to 2 years
- **Conservation Status:** Not Assessed

HABITAT & DIET

These spiders live in gardens, forests, and grasslands in temperate and tropical regions of Asia. They dine on a variety of insects.

FAMILY & SOCIAL LIFE

After mating, the female kills the male and lays her eggs in a sac. The baby spiders eat each other until the strongest spiderlings break through the sac.

DID YOU KNOW?

The zigzag pattern of the web helps to protect it from damage.

STICK INSECT

ALL ABOUT

The stick insect camouflages through mimicry. It looks like the twigs and branches on which it lives. This protects the stick insect from predators, such as spiders, rodents, and birds.

- **Length:** 1 to 12 inches (2.5 to 30.5 cm)
- **Weight:** not enough data
- **Lifespan:** up to 2 years
- **Conservation Status:** Not Assessed

HABITAT & DIET

Stick insects can be found in tropical forests and other areas rich with vegetation throughout southern Asia and Southeast Asia. They are herbivores and eat mostly leaves and plant matter.

FAMILY & SOCIAL LIFE

Eggs are laid on the underside of leaves, away from danger, or individually on the ground.

FUN FACT

The egg of a stick insect can still hatch after passing through the digestive tract of a bird.

WEAVER ANT

ALL ABOUT

Weaver ants are named for their tree nests that are woven together with leaves. Working in a chain, some ants hold the leaves together while other ants use silk secretions to glue the leaves in place.

- **Length:** up to 1 inch (2.5 cm)
- **Weight:** not enough data
- **Lifespan:** 8 to 10 weeks
- **Conservation Status:** Not Assessed

HABITAT & DIET

These ants are found in tropical rainforests of southern Asia and Southeast Asia. Their diet primarily consists of other insects.

FUN FACT

Weaver ants have been used for centuries in China to protect fruit trees from destructive insects.

FAMILY & SOCIAL LIFE

They live in large structured colonies that can have more than 500,000 workers. Colonies consist of a queen, workers, soldiers, and larvae.

ADDITIONAL INSECTS AND ARACHNIDS

ASIAN FOREST SCORPION

- **About:** Asian forest scorpions glow under ultraviolet light.
- **Habitat:** rainforest floor
- **Conservation Status:** Not Assessed

Asian forest scorpion

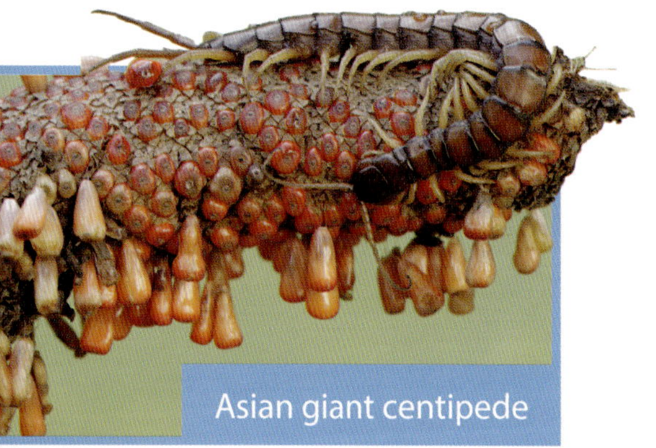
Asian giant centipede

ASIAN GIANT CENTIPEDE

- **About:** Giant centipedes use their numerous legs to capture and overcome prey.
- **Habitat:** tropical forests
- **Conservation Status:** Not Assessed

EAST ASIAN WOLF SPIDER

- **About:** Female wolf spiders attach egg sacs to their back and carry them until they hatch.
- **Habitat:** grasslands, wooded areas
- **Conservation Status:** Not Assessed

East Asian wolf spider

Fat-tailed scorpion

FAT-TAILED SCORPION

- **About:** When threatened, fat-tailed scorpions raise their tail to display their venomous stinger.
- **Habitat:** arid regions
- **Conservation Status:** Not Assessed

Jerusalem cricket

JERUSALEM CRICKET

- **About:** Jerusalem crickets are sometimes called potato bugs.
- **Habitat:** grasslands, woodlands, deserts
- **Conservation Status:** Vulnerable

TRAPDOOR SPIDER

- **About:** Trapdoor spiders construct elaborate burrows with hinged trapdoors made of silk and soil.
- **Habitat:** tropical regions
- **Conservation Status:** Not Assessed

Trapdoor spider

GLOSSARY

aerial
Taking place in the air.

alpha
The leader of a group of animals.

ambush
To make a surprise attack.

amphibious
Living both on land and in the water.

arboreal
Living mostly in trees.

arid
Very dry; having little or no rain.

arthropod
A type of animal with a segmented body, jointed limbs, and an exoskeleton.

bore
To dig a hole through or into something.

brackish
A bit salty.

buoyancy
The ability to float.

carrion
Dead and decaying flesh.

domestic
Living near or for the benefit of humans.

elusive
Secretive or hard to find.

Eurasia
The combined landmass of Europe and Asia.

monogamous
Mated with only one other animal at a time.

plumage
A bird's feather colors and patterns.

poacher
A person who hunts animals illegally.

ruminate
Chewing cud to then be redigested.

segmented
Separated into sections.

stallion
A male horse.

steppe
Wide, flat grassland with no trees.

toxin
A poison that causes harm when touched or swallowed.

trafficked
Sold illegally.

TO LEARN MORE

FURTHER READINGS

National Geographic, *Kids Animal Encyclopedia 2nd Edition*. National Geographic, 2021.

Spilsbury, Louise. *Saving the Asian Elephant*. Cheriton Children's Books, 2023.

Taylor-Butler, Christine, *Save the . . . Tigers*. Philomel Books, 2022.

Vanden Brande, Claire, *Asia*. Abdo, 2019.

ONLINE RESOURCES

To learn more about Asian animals, please visit **abdobooklinks.com** or scan this QR code. These links are routinely monitored and updated to provide the most current information available.

INDEX

PHOTO CREDITS

Cover Photos: Dmitry Potashkin/iStock/Getty Images, front (markhor); Wirestock Creators/Shutterstock, front (Asian green bee-eater); Kletr/Shutterstock, front (Asian elephant); monster_code/iStock/Getty Images, front (Indian flower mantis); Eric Isselee/Shutterstock, front (clouded leopard), back (Komodo dragon); kongsky/Shutterstock, front (gecko); reptiles4all/Shutterstock, front (jerboa), front (Indian star tortoise); Hung Chung Chih/Shutterstock, front (giant panda); fotoslaz/Shutterstock, front (Siberian tiger); Kurit afshen/Shutterstock, front (Asian common toad); marshalgonz/Shutterstock, back (Indian bison); beejung/Shutterstock, back (green pit viper)
Interior Photos: Dmitri Gomon/Shutterstock, 1, 26, 36 (bottom); MariaMaslova/Shutterstock, 2–3, 109 (bottom); Vladimir Wrangel/Shutterstock, 4; Picture by Tambako the Jaguar/Moment/Getty Images, 5; kv naushad/Shutterstock, 6; Designua/Shutterstock, 7; PhotocechCZ/Shutterstock, 8; Suvorov_Alex/Shutterstock, 9, 44; Merrillie Redden/Shutterstock, 10; Westend61/Getty Images, 11; Nigel Hicks/NHPA/Photoshot/Newscom, 12; Ranjan Barthakur/Shutterstock, 13; Raghupathi K.V./500px/Getty Images, 14; Natursports/Shutterstock, 15 (top); Nilanka Sampath/iStock/Getty Images, 15 (bottom); Tigger11th/Shutterstock, 16; Dgwildlife/iStock/Getty Images, 17; PHOTO BY LOLA/Shutterstock, 18; clkraus/Shutterstock, 19; Martin Mecnarowski/Shutterstock, 20, 30; Wi Holy/Shutterstock, 21; scigelova/Shutterstock, 22; Photo Spirit/Shutterstock, 23; Vadim Balakin/500px/500Px Plus/Getty Images, 24; Byrdyak/iStock/Getty Images, 25; Kshitij30/Shutterstock, 27; Eric Isselee/Shutterstock, 28; Lubomir Novak/Shutterstock, 29; Sourabh Bharti/Shutterstock, 31, 128; Kjetil Kolbjornsrud/Shutterstock, 32; clarst5/Shutterstock, 33; Ondrej Prosicky/Shutterstock, 34; Jan Stria/Shutterstock, 35; Subair Cheerathodi/Shutterstock, 36 (top); Sharon Morris/Shutterstock, 37 (top); T99Image/Shutterstock, 37 (middle); Schafer & Hill/The Image Bank/Getty Images, 37 (bottom); aleksander hunta/Shutterstock, 38, 51; BirdHunter591/iStock/Getty Images, 39; Yantar/Shutterstock, 40; Sergei25/Shutterstock, 41 (top); ePhotocorp/iStock/Getty Images, 41 (bottom), 95; MrZeroman/Shutterstock, 42; Nick Pecker/Shutterstock, 43; longtaildog/Shutterstock, 45; neelsky/Shutterstock, 46; FadiBarghouthy/Shutterstock, 47; EsHanPhot/Shutterstock, 48; Hung Chung Chih/Shutterstock, 49; The Escape of Malee/Shutterstock, 50; Kurit afshen/Shutterstock, 52, 81 (bottom), 170 (bottom), 173 (top), 174; Plutonian_p/Shutterstock, 53; Roland IJdema/Shutterstock, 54; Ruchith Jayathilake/Shutterstock, 55; Syuhada Sapno/Shutterstock, 56; Edwin Butter/Shutterstock, 57; Lauren Bilboe/Shutterstock, 58; jeep2499/Shutterstock, 59; Don Mammoser/Shutterstock, 60; Wang LiQiang/Shutterstock, 61 (top), 79 (bottom), 111; Dani Jara/Shutterstock, 61 (bottom); Yakov Oskanov/Shutterstock, 62; sommai patpan/Shutterstock, 63; BirdSulfuric/Shutterstock, 64; Ben Queenborough/Shutterstock, 65 (top); brucelin/Shutterstock, 65 (bottom); K. Nakao/Shutterstock, 66; Lauren Suryanata/Shutterstock, 67, 80; teekayu/Shutterstock, 68; CRS PHOTO/Shutterstock, 69 (top); dwi putra stock/Shutterstock, 69 (bottom), 102; dimcha/Shutterstock, 70; Avustfel/Wikimedia Commons, 71; kajornyot wildlife photography/Shutterstock, 72; arthur_ensis/iNaturalist, 73; Christian Musat/Shutterstock, 74, 139; CameraBaba/Shutterstock, 75; KakerNaturepic/Shutterstock, 76; ANDREI RASPUTIN/Shutterstock, 77; Katoosha/Shutterstock, 78 (top); aDam Wildlife/Shutterstock, 78 (middle), 149 (top), 154 (top), 154 (bottom); vkilikov/Shutterstock, 78 (bottom); scott mirror/Shutterstock, 79 (top); PACO COMO/Shutterstock, 79 (middle), 123; Ruben PH/Shutterstock, 81 (top); Julien Viry/iStock/Getty Images, 82 (top); Mikhail Blajenov/Shutterstock, 82 (bottom); Danny Ye/Shutterstock, 83, 133, 148; Milan Zygmunt/Shutterstock, 84; Ton Ponchai/Shutterstock, 85, 103, 108 (bottom); GoodFocused/Shutterstock, 86; I Wayan Sumatika/Shutterstock, 87, 100, 186 (top), 186 (middle); Erni/Shutterstock, 88, 158 (top); GUDKOV ANDREY/Shutterstock, 89; Rajendra Parkar/Shutterstock, 90; johnaudrey/iStock/Getty Images, 91; Banjong Khanyai/Shutterstock, 92 (top); SAHAI IMAGE/Shutterstock, 92 (bottom); RupaeshAgarwaal/Shutterstock, 93; Skynavin/Shutterstock, 94; Paul Tessier/Shutterstock, 96; Girish HC/Shutterstock, 97 (top); Mufti Adi Utomo/Shutterstock, 97 (bottom); beejung/Shutterstock, 98; lisdiyanto suhardjo/Shutterstock, 99; Phornsiri/Shutterstock, 101; Lutsenko_Oleksandr/Shutterstock, 104; MicExplore/Shutterstock, 105; orlandin/Shutterstock, 106; Rawlinson_Photography/E+/Getty Images, 107 (top); NaturePicsFilms/Shutterstock, 107 (bottom); Soumyabrata Roy/NurPhoto/Getty Images, 108 (top); Shyjo/Shutterstock, 108 (middle); Chattraphas Pongcharoen/Shutterstock, 109 (top); kuritafsheen/RooM/Getty Images, 109 (middle); Dutchieworldtravel/Shutterstock, 110; wuttidanai/Shutterstock, 112; Vaclav Matous/Shutterstock, 113, 114, 116; Michal Lukaszewicz/Shutterstock, 115 (top); Tareq Uddin Ahmed/Shutterstock, 115 (bottom); Guoqiang Xue/Shutterstock, 117; Sunil Onamkulam/Shutterstock, 118; SergeBertasiusPhotography/Shutterstock, 119; Evgeny Gi/Shutterstock, 120; Hit1912/Shutterstock, 121; smutan/Shutterstock, 122; Steven Gill/Shutterstock, 124; Mehd M. Halaouate/Shutterstock, 125; AntonChepigin/Shutterstock, 126 (top); Adam Yee/Shutterstock, 126 (bottom); rock ptarmigan/Shutterstock, 127; chuyu/iStock/Getty Images, 129; Agami Photo Agency/Shutterstock, 130; D. Longenbaugh/Shutterstock, 131; Karel Bartik/Shutterstock, 132; kojihirano/Shutterstock, 134; Belozorova Elena/Shutterstock, 135 (top); Daniel Danckwerts/Shutterstock, 135 (bottom); rofeeq.birdinghimalayas/Shutterstock, 136; Wichyanan Limparungpatthanakij/iStock/Getty Images, 137; AMARJEETSINH JHALA/Shutterstock, 138; SunflowerMomma/Shutterstock, 140; Risto Puranen/Shutterstock, 141; Wirestock Creators/Shutterstock, 142, 166 (bottom); CameraGuy305/Shutterstock, 143 (top); viraj bavarva/Shutterstock, 143 (bottom); Photo by K S Kong/Moment Open/Getty Images, 144; a_v_d/Shutterstock, 145; Sacharewicz Patryk/Shutterstock, 146 (top); Guy Gabovich/Shutterstock, 146 (bottom); ZakiFF/Shutterstock, 147 (top); Kersti Lindstrom/Shutterstock, 147 (middle); Hanne and Jens Eriksen/NPL/Minden Pictures, 147 (bottom); atartusi/Shutterstock, 149 (bottom); SandmanPhotography/Shutterstock, 150 (top); Daniel Lamborn/Shutterstock, 150 (bottom); Nicholas Toh/Shutterstock, 151 (top); Kamal Hari Menon/Shutterstock, 151 (bottom); Roman Choknadii/Shutterstock, 152; DiveSpin.Com/Shutterstock, 153; Guido Montaldo/Shutterstock, 155 (top); feathercollector/Shutterstock, 155 (bottom); Andrei Armiagov/Shutterstock, 156; Richard Whitcombe/Shutterstock, 157; Marek Mierzejewski/Shutterstock, 158 (middle); Olha Solodenko/Shutterstock, 158 (bottom); Juan Vega Underwater/Shutterstock, 159 (top); Miroslav Halama/Shutterstock, 159 (middle); Rostislav Stefanek/Shutterstock, 159 (bottom); pittaya/Shutterstock, 160; tristan tan/Shutterstock, 161 (top), 164; ichihira/Shutterstock, 161 (bottom), 166 (top); ossyugioh/iStock/Getty Images, 162; Rama Narayanan/iNaturalist, 163; Agung Widiyanto/Shutterstock, 165; Martin Voeller/Shutterstock, 167; Paul Starosta/Stone/Getty Images, 168; lessysebastian/Shutterstock, 169; Tooro42/Shutterstock, 170 (top); Rudmer Zwerver/Shutterstock, 170 (middle); Petr Bambousek/Shutterstock, 171 (top); Gerry Bishop/Shutterstock, 171 (middle); HWall/Shutterstock, 171 (bottom); KRIACHKO OLEKSII/Shutterstock, 172; Chase D'animulls/Shutterstock, 173 (bottom); Ruzy Hartini/Shutterstock, 175 (top); asharkyu/Shutterstock, 175 (bottom); Rod Williams/Shutterstock, 176; DiamondWarriors/Shutterstock, 177; Wacpan/Dreamstime.com, 178; Riccardo Arata/Shutterstock, 179; monster_code/Shutterstock, 180; Arjun9810/Shutterstock, 181; Sumit sanit/Shutterstock, 182; Avinash Deo/Shutterstock, 183; Stephane Bidouze/Shutterstock, 184 (top); cynoclub/Shutterstock, 184 (bottom); Dewiq's Art/Shutterstock, 185; Yunhyok Choi/Shutterstock, 186 (bottom); Ernie Cooper/Shutterstock, 187 (top); Quyen Tat/Shutterstock, 187 (middle); Pong Wira/Shutterstock, 187 (bottom)

ABDOBOOKS.COM

Published by Abdo Reference, a division of ABDO, PO Box 398166, Minneapolis, Minnesota 55439.

Printed in China
052025
092025

Editor: Jane Katirgis
Series Designer: Colleen McLaren

LIBRARY OF CONGRESS CONTROL NUMBER: 2024949014

PUBLISHER'S CATALOGING-IN-PUBLICATION DATA

Names: Basu, Ritta M., author.
Title: The Asian animal encyclopedia / by Ritta M. Basu
Description: Minneapolis, Minnesota : Abdo Reference, 2026 | Series: Animal encyclopedias | Includes online resources and index.
Identifiers: ISBN 9781098296599 (lib. bdg.) | ISBN 9798384918028 (ebook)
Subjects: LCSH: Zoology--Juvenile literature. | Animals--Juvenile literature. | Animals--Behavior--Juvenile literature. | Animal habitats--Juvenile literature. | Reference materials--Juvenile literature. | Encyclopedias and dictionaries--Juvenile literature.
Classification: DDC 590.3--dc23